THE RED LION INN COOKBOOK

STOCKBRIDGE LIBRARY ASSOCIATION HISTORICAL ROOM

An 1829 drawing of the Main Street of Stockbridge by Electa Webster. The Red Lion Inn is on the right, much smaller than it is today.

THE RED LION INN COOKBOOK

Suzi Forbes Chase

THE RED LION INN

BERKSHIRE HOUSE, Publishers
STOCKBRIDGE, MASSACHUSETTS

We gratefully acknowledge permission from the following publishers to use excerpts from the following authors:

American Cookery, James Beard, copyright 1972, Little, Brown and Company; *The American Heritage Cookbook,* by The Editors of American Heritage, the Magazine of History, copyright 1964, 1969; *General Foods Cookbook,* by The Women of General Foods Kitchens, copyright 1959, Random House; *New England Cookbook*, Eleanor Early, copyright 1954, Random House, Inc.

Edited by Katherine G. Ness and Sarah Novak
Cover and page design by Jane McWhorter
Typesetting and page layout by Phil Ruderman
Production services by Ripinsky & Company and Quality Printing

Color photography: Color photography between pages 116 and 117 by Craig Hammell; view of Red Lion Inn room with breakfast, courtesy of The Red Lion Inn.

Library of Congress Cataloging-in-Publication Data

Chase, Suzi Forbes
    The Red Lion Inn cookbook / Suzi Forbes Chase.
        p. cm.
    Includes bibliographical references and index.
    ISBN 0-936399-29-5 (cloth) : $24.95. -- ISBN 0-936399-28-7 (paper):
$14.95
    1. Cookery, American--New England style.   2. Red Lion Inn
(Stockbridge, Mass.) I. Title.
TX715.2.N48C44 1992
641.5974—dc20   92-23780
                                           CIP

ISBN 0-936399-29-5, cloth
ISBN 0-936399-28-7, paper

10 9 8 7 6 5 4 3
Printed in Mexico by R.R. Donnelley & Sons Company

To M.D.C.

ACKNOWLEDGMENTS

My first visit to The Red Lion Inn was in 1972 — and it was love at first sight. The history that permeates every nook and cranny left me longing to learn more. Each time I visited — truly one of my favorite places — I hoped to find a Red Lion Inn cookbook to take home as a reminder of my memorable meals. So when my husband and I moved to Stockbridge in 1987, I began discussing the possibility of writing one — and at last the possibility is a reality.

I owe special thanks to so many people. To Jane and Jack Fitzpatrick, for encouraging the project and for allowing their staff to participate. To Betsy Holtzinger, Red Lion Inn innkeeper, for hiring such talented people, and for her keen design sense that proved so helpful throughout the project.

To Chef Steven Mongeon, I will be eternally grateful. He spent hours converting recipes from hotel quantities to home quantities — and that's no small task. He tested and retested recipes in the Red Lion Inn kitchen and in his home, and he gave invaluable guidance to our official recipe testers. I gained great respect for Chef Mongeon's profound knowledge. He is a virtual encyclopedia of culinary information — from the broadest concept to the smallest detail.

Special thanks also to Pastry Chef Marcia Kneisel, who converted all the breads and desserts to home-sized quantities. After all, what would most homes do with 25 loaves of Red Lion Inn Lemon Bread?

My very special thanks to Dennis Barquinero, Director of Lodging at The Red Lion Inn. He had the task of coordinating the project for all divisions of the inn, and his assistance was invaluable. With Dennis around, anything is do-able. His attention to detail and solid good judgment were absolutely essential ingredients, and his unfailing cheerfulness and cooperative spirit made the project a joy.

The recipe testers, Miriam Jacobs and Georgeanne Rousseau, patiently and professionally corrected ingredients and suggested simplified ways of expressing directions — and always with a cheerful sense of humor. Dinners at the Rousseau's (always with such stimulating conversation), as we tasted some of the results, were an extra dividend for Dustin and me. Katherine G. Ness, our cookbook editor, whipped the entire book into excellent shape, ensuring consistency, continuity, and accuracy.

Craig Hammel, the photographer, brought not only his cameras, but also his artistic eye and attention to details. He found in every corner of the inn the perfect props to re-create the unique Red Lion ambience and to provide the ideal background for the food.

Jane McWhorter, the book's designer, brought her elegant style to the page and cover design; Phil Ruderman, typesetter, carried through that style and elegance on every page. At Berkshire House, Mary Osak efficiently managed so many editorial details, and all the traffic of material back and forth to The Red Lion Inn — always with efficiency and good humor. And Polly Pierce, who presides over the Stockbridge Library Association Historical Room with such charm and grace, helped immeasurably with many of the wonderful historic photographs in these pages.

To Jean Rousseau and David Emblidge, who believed in this project all along, and made it happen — what can I say? Faced with a short deadline, a small staff, and a tight budget, they always said, "We can do this — it will be great!" And we did, and it is.

At dinner, I always save the best for last. And that's what I've done here too. My greatest thanks go to my editor, Sarah Novak. She unerringly knew exactly when to cut and when to add, and when to leave it be. It was wonderfully reassuring to know I could always trust her judgment and count on her commitment. Thank you, Sarah, for your decisiveness, your very hard work, and your good cheer always.

The book has been an absolute joy for me from beginning to end — made so by the unfailing support I received. My sincere and heartfelt thanks to you all.

S.F.C.

Dear Friend,

The Red Lion Inn has been an important part of our life here in Stockbridge for a long time. It's been a landmark for travelers since 1773, and home to Country Curtains since we bought it 25 years ago.

For those of you who haven't had a chance to visit, we can tell you that The Red Lion Inn is a great big New England inn. Our guests love relaxing on our long front porch that faces Main Street. Around back is a quiet courtyard for dining surrounded by lush impatiens and trees. The guest rooms upstairs are filled with antiques ... and the dining room with an ambience of country elegance and welcome. We think it's wonderful!

We are delighted to bring a part of The Red Lion Inn to you. This Red Lion Inn Cookbook, written by our neighbor Suzi Forbes Chase, celebrates the time-tested, kitchen-proven recipes of Chef Steve who has been with us at the Inn for 12 years.

We know you and your family will love our traditional New England specialities and delicious contemporary dishes as much as our guests do.

Thank you for your interest in our new cookbook!

Most sincerely,

Jane & Jack Fitzpatrick

CONTENTS

THE HISTORY OF THE RED LION INN

THE RED LION INN
Fine Food and Lodging Since 1773.
Stockbridge, Mass. 01262 413-298-5545

Although the Mayflower landed at Plymouth in the Massachusetts Bay Colony in 1620, it was another century before Stockbridge in western Massachusetts was settled. In 1736, John Sergeant, missionary to the Indians, established the first crude settlement at a horseshoe bend in the serpentine Housatonic River in western Massachusetts. In merely three years, however, the tiny village was considered permanent enough for incorporation, adopting the name of Stockbridge, after the town of the same name in Hampshire County, England.

Stockbridge was on the post road from Albany to Boston. As horseback travel increased, so did the necessity to feed and house the weary traveler. Thus taverns were established along its length, The Red Lion Inn among them. Eventually, the crude trails were widened to accommodate stagecoaches, and tavern business steadily increased.

Norman Simpson, a Berkshire County resident and author, explained the proliferation of these taverns in a 1971 article in the *Boston Globe*. "In Puritan Massachusetts 'ordinaries' (taverns) were established as quickly as churches in new communities. A 1656 proclamation by the General Court fined towns without public houses.... Taverns, in which news from the outside world was daily posted and discussed, were truer town centers than the church or village green."

Allan Forbes and Ralph M. Eastman describe the typical tavern in their delightful book *Taverns and Stagecoaches of New England.* "Coaches usually traveled at the rate of four or five miles an hour with a change of horses every ten miles. This gave passengers the opportunity to refresh themselves at the taverns along the way. It was customary for the stage to arrive at an inn at the hour of noon when a hearty dinner, the chief meal of the day, was ready for the travelers. When it came to overnight lodging, there was no such thing as a private room. All beds were big enough to accommodate at least two persons and frequently there were as many as three beds in a room. The tavern keeper did not consider his house filled until every bed was yielding at least double income. If a guest wanted a bath or a fire in the room, there was an extra charge. The fire was kindled to order in the fireplace, or stove, and the bath was taken in a wooden tub which a porter filled with hot water carried up from the kitchen."

The busy Albany-Boston turnpike spawned many taverns and stagecoach stops, and The Red Lion Inn became one of the most popular. Most historians place its birth at 1773. The inn was built by Silas Pepoon, who named his establishment the Stockbridge Tavern. He distinguished it by hanging a colorful sign featuring a shiny red lion with a bright green tail. The tavern quickly gained popularity — and renown as well. In 1774 Pepoon's tavern was the site of a county-wide convention to protest the use of British goods. The document the attendees produced has been called "America's First Declaration of Independence."

When the prominent jurist Theodore Sedgwick moved to Stockbridge with his family in 1785, there was limited stagecoach travel, although horseback travel and private carriages were frequent. His daughter Catherine Sedgwick, destined to become the first acclaimed American woman author, wrote that "there were no steamers, no railroads, and a stage route through our valley but once a week. Gentlemen made their journeys in private carriages. Yet, insidiously, the outer world was creeping in," Ms. Sedgwick lamented.

Stagecoach travel steadily increased, to three times a week by 1807, then to once a day, and eventually to eight times a day — four in each direction, stopping for a rest and change of horses at the Stockbridge Tavern.

The Red Lion Inn served stagecoach travelers on the Albany-Boston turnpike.

CRAIG HAMMELL

In 1807 Pepoon sold his tavern to Anna Bingham. The inn she presided over was small, with low ceilings, heavy beams, and massive supporting posts in the dining room, looking then much as "Widow Bingham's Tavern" does today, with its cozy pub-like atmosphere. A great, open fireplace contained a blazing fire in the winter. Eight bedrooms on the second floor sheltered overnight guests and, on the top floor, the ballroom was used for assemblies and meetings, as well as festive parties.

Widow Bingham sold the inn to Daniel Pepoon and in 1822 he sold it to Jonathan Hicks. For the next forty years, the tavern's fortunes were meager. To a proper English family that moved to Stockbridge in the 1820s, temporarily staying at J. Hicks' Inn, it seemed uncivilized, coarse, and almost barbarian. The daughter, Anne Ashburner, wrote that "the red-faced owner, Mr. Hicks, and his fat, good-natured wife seemed the essence of vulgarity and just the persons to keep such an inn."

However, with the Sedgwicks in town, the social and intellectual scene buzzed. In 1835 the famous English actress Fanny Kemble came to Stockbridge to visit with Catherine Sedgwick, eventually making nearby Lenox her home — despite her claim that there was no good bread in all of Berkshire County. (She sent Catherine a recipe for "effervescing bread" to overcome this flaw.)

And then the railroad came. As early as 1826 Theodore Sedgwick had proposed a railroad through Stockbridge, but progress was slow. In 1838, however, the Hudson-Berkshire Railroad completed a three-mile spur from Stateline, New York, to West Stockbridge, so for twelve years passengers bound for The Red Lion Inn arrived at the tiny depot in West Stockbridge. Finally, in 1850, the Berkshire branch of the New Haven & Hartford Railroad from New York was finished, depositing throngs of people at the Stockbridge station every summer. Eventually two express trains made the trip daily, in four hours.

In 1848 the *Pittsfield Sun* described the inn, now named the Stockbridge House: "[It] contains four pleasant and airy Parlours, a spacious Dining Hall, and thirty-four large and well ventilated rooms. Bathing Rooms are attached to the House.... A Superior Livery Stable is attached to the House and horses and carriages will be ready at a moment's notice and for moderate charge."

The mid-19th century abounded with literary visitors to The Red Lion Inn. William Cullen Bryant was born in Berkshire County and practiced law in Great Barrington, and returned to the Berkshires frequently. In 1850, Nathaniel Hawthorne came to Stockbridge looking "for a cheap, pleasant, and healthy residence." Hawthorne had just written *The Scarlet Letter,* and was offered a small red house at the north end of the Stockbridge Bowl, in a location that must have seemed extremely remote at the time. Nevertheless, Herman Melville, who owned a house some eight miles distant in Pittsfield, walked over to visit Hawthorne often. It was here that Hawthorne wrote *The House of Seven Gables*, among other tales.

Oliver Wendell Holmes and Henry Wadsworth Longfellow came, too, both occupying homes in Pittsfield, and probably taking many meals at The Red

Lion Inn. In 1853 Henry Ward Beecher owned a nearby house, where he spent several summers.

In the two-hundred-year-plus history of The Red Lion Inn, fortune seems to have brought saviors to the door just when the inn's destiny seemed least promising. In 1862 the inn was purchased by Mr. and Mrs. Charles H. Plumb, and a family tenure that extended three generations — a 90-year span from the Plumbs, to their nephew Allen T. Treadway, to his son Heaton I. Treadway — brought prosperity and stability to the inn. Charles and "Aunt Mert," as she was called, lavished attention and love on the old inn.

Aunt Mert knew antiques and with a practiced eye roamed the countryside, rescuing treasures for the Stockbridge House parlors, bedrooms, and dining rooms. Reputedly, the first antique purchased for the inn was the magnificent grandfather clock that stands today beside the elevator. It is dated 1790 and, the story goes, was purchased for $10. Another notable antique is the large mahogany table that once served as the dining room table in New York's Union League Club, said to have been dined at by Thackeray, Lincoln, and Dickens, among others. It now holds a place of prominence in the center of the lobby.

With a droll sense of humor, Heaton Treadway described many of the antiques in "The Tale of the Lion" — witty tales told by the Red Lion himself (whether they are truth or pure fiction, we'll never know). They were published originally on the back of the Sunday menus, and later printed in a pamphlet. The tales contain whimsical accounts of Aunt Mert's discoveries, such as the following: "Some of us speculate in stocks, some of us in Florida real estate, and I limit mine to buying and collecting second-hand furniture and I haven't done too badly. The sideboard in the back of the dining room is a remarkable piece in that it has the original maker's label on each of the cabinet doors. It was found by 'Aunt Mert' being used as a chicken coop. She paid $3.50 for this piece of second-hand junk. It is a piece of Hepplewhite and was made by William Whitehead, Cabinet and Chair Maker,

A view of Mrs. Plumb's private parlor, 1894, in the inn then known as Stockbridge House.

Pearl Street, New York City. It is his card that is pasted on the inside of the cabinet doors." The sideboard continues to grace the inn today.

Word spread quickly through the countryside that "Aunt Mert" would pay "fifty cents for any teapot and a dollar for any mirror." Many of the teapots that line the parlors, and the mirrors in the hallways and bedrooms, were brought to The Red Lion Inn from neighboring farms and houses. Then as now, however, the priceless antique collection adorns the inn for the enjoyment of the guests. When asked why such valuable antiques are used, Mr. Treadway once replied, "You must remember that the inn is the home of the guest. In his own home he admires his antiques and other objects of art at his own pleasure. It is our desire that he enjoy the same freedom and pleasure at the inn."

In 1884 the Plumbs increased the inn's size to accommodate up to one hundred guests. They equipped each room with a Franklin stove or fireplace, which was lighted every evening to ward off the chill. In 1893 they added yet another wing and a new dining room. And then disaster struck.

On August 31, 1896, a fire started in the pastry kitchen and soon spread throughout the inn. Flames engulfed room after room, until only a black skeleton of Stockbridge House remained. Fortunately, there were no injuries, and townsfolk formed a brigade to save the collections of furniture, pictures, colonial china, teapots, mirrors, and clothes.

Undaunted, the Treadways and Plumbs immediately rebuilt the inn and a mere eight months later an elegant new building rose from the ashes. Christened The Red Lion Inn, it was larger, grander, and safer than the old, although it retained the colonial charm of the original.

Praise and acclaim attended the opening of the new inn. It was noted that brick fire stops had been placed between partitions to prevent a similar conflagration in the future. A thoughtful addition to the new inn was the special "women's door" that led to a women's reception room and parlor. A women's retiring room at the far end of the entrance hall was used by women who had journeyed to the inn for the day only.

A chapter in *Taverns and Stagecoaches of New England* describes the rebuilt Red Lion Inn: "When the present building was constructed, it was in a period when it was considered unsanitary to sleep in a room adjoining a toilet. Because of this only two private bath rooms were provided in the whole

"All that is left of it is a portion of the front part, which is of no use, and will simply have to be torn down. The hotel was insured for $20,000, and the contents for $5,000. The loss is estimated at fully $50,000. It was the most disastrous fire that ever visited the town. The fire was discovered at 4:30 a.m. by the night watchman. He discovered flames bursting forth from the pastry kitchen in the rear of the house."

The Berkshire Evening Eagle, "Stockbridge Inn Gone" August 31, 1896

"At The Red Lion Inn, the middle of the week saw something over seventy guests registered and the arrivals during the past three days brought the number up to more than 120. There are a number of brides and grooms among the guests and some of them have shown remarkable accomplishments as pedestrians. It seems to be a common thing for them to walk up to Lenox or to Monument Mountain summit and other long things are taken to the evident enjoyment of the young people...."

Berkshire Resort Topics, 1904

President Franklin Delano Roosevelt's signature in The Red Lion Inn's guest book.

establishment. It was customary then for season guests to bring their own bath tubs and it was nothing out of the ordinary after the arrival of the evening train to have to deliver twenty or twenty-five bath tubs an evening to the rooms, along with trunks and other luggage. The natural sequence was not too much appreciated by the maids of the inn as they had to take on the onerous duty of carrying hot water to the various rooms which harbored the traveling bath tubs."

The new inn boasted larger dining rooms, grander parlors and reception rooms, a total of twenty-two fireplaces, and eighty guest rooms. The grand "piazza" (we call it the front porch today) extended the length of the inn, right on Main Street, and was placed high enough above street level that Joseph Choate, a prominent New York lawyer, who summered in Stockbridge, was led to remark, "If anyone sat long enough on the Red Lion veranda he would see pass everybody worth knowing." That would have included President William McKinley, who came to Stockbridge shortly after the new inn opened, to wish Choate well in his new position as U.S. Ambassador to Great Britain.

Even this new, modern inn, however, was not equipped with central heating (nor were the elaborate summer "cottages" built by wealthy New Yorkers in the surrounding hills). The inn would open each April and close sometime in November. Rachel Field, an author from a prominent Stockbridge family, remarked, "It was winter not so much when the first snow fell as when The Red Lion Inn put up its shutters, after the departure of the last city visitor." An attempt to open the inn year-round as recently as 1960 failed, and the famous 1967 painting by Stockbridge resident Norman Rockwell called "Stockbridge at Christmas" shows a dark, shuttered Red Lion Inn hibernating through the winter months.

Touring cars were the mode of transportation to the inn by 1900, and a stately procession of elegant automobiles could be seen parked in front of the grand "piazza."

In 1935 Mrs. Calvin (Grace) Coolidge, wife of the late former president, was the first to sign the guest book for the summer season. A humorous story is told about Calvin Coolidge. It seems that while still a Massachusetts official, he had come to the inn to give a speech in nearby Great Barrington, but when his party arrived at the speech site, they couldn't find Cal. He had been left behind at The Red Lion Inn, where he was found calmly waiting on the front porch. Presidents Cleveland, McKinley, Van

Buren, Theodore Roosevelt, and Franklin D. Roosevelt have also stayed at the inn.

Royalty made their way to The Red Lion Inn as well. The Prince of Liechtenstein visited in 1934, when he had the misfortune to lose several of his royal handkerchiefs, according to an article in the *Berkshire Eagle*. "It seems the Prince had the habit of dropping soiled 'kerchiefs in his wastepaper basket, and then forgetting about the outcome. He supposed they were carted off to the laundry. The floor maid, however, had other ideas about handkerchiefs in wastebaskets, so to the incinerator they went. Thus, the royal linen underwent a shortage during the week."

The arrival of a new resident to Stockbridge in 1953 brought to the village and to The Red Lion Inn continuing recognition and acclaim. Norman Rockwell, famed illustrator and creator of many *Saturday Evening Post* covers, moved to Stockbridge. From that day on, Stockbridge residents became the models for a variety of *Post* illustrations, from the country doctor to schoolteachers, to policemen, and to children. Signed first printings and artist proofs of many of those illustrations line the hallways and public rooms of The Red Lion Inn today, and every guest room has at least one Rockwell print. The Norman Rockwell Museum in Stockbridge has the largest collection of original Rockwell paintings in the world. Some of the guides at the museum are former models for Rockwell paintings, and they highlight their tours with personal anecdotes and memories.

Perhaps of equal importance to The Red Lion Inn, however, is the publishing company begun by Norman Simpson in the early 1960s: The Berkshire Traveller Press. His first publication was a chatty, humorous description of visits to several inns by Mr. Simpson, as "The Berkshire Traveller." The Red Lion Inn was always on top of his personal list of favorites, and when his tiny pamphlet blossomed into an acclaimed series of guides to inns and bed and breakfast establishments — the first of its kind — it acquainted travelers around the world with The Red Lion Inn. *Country Inns and Back Roads*, now published by HarperCollins, still continues to lure travelers to The Red Lion's door. Berkshire Traveller Press is now an imprint of Berkshire House.

It was in 1968 that a new savior for The Red Lion Inn arrived on the scene. The Treadways had attempted, unsuccessfully, to sell the inn in 1955. Robert K. Wheeler, owner of an insurance company and a conscientious local

COUNTRY CURTAINS
STOCKBRIDGE
MASSACHUSETTS
01262

"For fifty years I have enjoyed The Red Lion Inn's hospitality. Time after time I have been told that it would no longer be there next year; but Lord be praised, it's still there, and I hope it will be as delightful and congenial for another fifty years, for one way or another, I'll be happily there."

Thornton Wilder, comment in the Red Lion Inn's guest book, December 30, 1972

The Reverend Alfred B. Starrett, former rector of St. Paul's Episcopal Church, directly across Main Street from The Red Lion Inn, penned this poem in 1951. He added the final stanza in 1973 to celebrate the inn's bicentennial.

"It takes a heap of living in an Inn to make it right,
A heap of sun and shadow, both the sad days and
*   the bright.*
It takes a lot of caring for the welfare of the guests
To know, before they ask you, how to answer their
*   requests.*
It's not the chairs and tables nor the shingles on
*   the roof,*
But the wanting others happy that furnishes the
*   proof.*

A real Inn can't be bought, or built, or made up in
*   a minute,*
To make an Inn there's got to be a heap of living in
*   it.*
The singing and the laughter have to work into the
*   wood,*
And stoves get used to cooking so that meals are
*   downright good.*
The staff must fit together as a smoothly working
*   whole*
Through the long cooperation there of every single
*   soul.*

You need good beds and linens, and a lovely village
*   too,*
But the things that really matter are the old things,
*   not the new; –*
The age-old smile of welcome and the well-worn
*   wish to please,*
The years of long experience that put a guest at
*   ease,*
The gracious hospitality for travelers who roam,

(continued on next page)

citizen, finally purchased it in 1960. Despairing over the cost of upkeep, he diligently looked for an owner who would transform the inn into a 20th-century hostelry. In 1968, his dream was realized when he sold it to the current owners, John and Jane Fitzpatrick, local residents who operated a thriving curtain mail order business, called Country Curtains.

The Fitzpatricks brought with them a renewed interest in the antiques collection, an allegiance to the historic significance of Stockbridge, a commitment to restore the inn, and an appreciation for superior food and service. Foremost among the capital improvements was the installation of central heating, allowing the inn to remain open throughout the year; and a steady increase in the number of modern bathrooms, so that almost all rooms now have private baths. A former lounge was turned into the Widow Bingham's Tavern, a modern kitchen was installed, and the inn today enjoys the amenities of a modern hotel within a historic structure. In 1983, the quaint Victorian iron lace elevator in the lobby was restored, and converted from a water to an oil hydraulic system, allowing it to remain in use year-round.

The Fitzpatricks originally converted a wing of the inn to administrative offices for Country Curtains, but today, the wing once again houses overnight guests of the inn (although a Country Curtains shop selling curtains, gifts, and bedding is located on the main floor). The administration, warehouse, and general offices of the business are located elsewhere.

Formal dining at The Red Lion Inn takes place in the Main Dining Room, lined with priceless paintings and filled with antiques. Informal dining takes place in the Widow Bingham's Tavern or downstairs in the Lion's Den, which also offers late night entertainment. In summer, the courtyard, filled with bright impatiens and umbrellaed tables under the spreading elm trees, is the popular choice for meals.

Famed guests continue to make the pilgrimage to The Red Lion Inn. John Wayne stayed at the inn in 1973, while Norman Rockwell painted his portrait for the National Cowboy Hall of Fame in Oklahoma City. He became a familiar sight in below-freezing weather, striding across the porch in a cowboy hat, and a Western cut suit with a kerchief at his neck. At one point an amateur photographer took too long to focus his camera on him and Wayne exclaimed, "Fire that thing, boy — fire!"

In the 1970s Norman Mailer lived nearby, and William Shirer and Arthur Penn still do. Thornton Wilder stayed and wrote at the inn every summer for 50 years. Stars on the boards of the Berkshire Theatre Festival, just down the street, make their temporary home at The Red Lion Inn each summer. Paul Newman and Joanne Woodward came in 1977, and several times since, and Richard Chamberlain was a guest in 1978. J. Daniel Travanti stayed at the inn in 1987, Julie Harris in 1988, and Teresa Wright many times.

Tanglewood, the summer home of the Boston Symphony Orchestra, is just up the road, so famed conductors, artists, and composers are frequent visitors too. Leonard Bernstein, Arthur Fiedler, John Williams, Itzhak Perlman, and many others have stayed at The Red Lion Inn. The lovely cottages surrounding the main building are ideal accommodations for musicians who like to rehearse in privacy.

In 1975 TV newsman David Brinkley thanked the inn for his comfortable stay and for treating him as an "ordinary" guest. TV personality Gene Shalit frequently visits the inn where he has obviously learned to cope with his easily recognizable features by wearing a T-shirt that reads: "No I'm not ... I just look like him." TV news personality Hugh Downs and his wife, and actress Maureen Stapleton, are frequent diners. That's just the way it is at The Red Lion Inn.

The Red Lion Inn is a historic treasure that survived from a quieter, gentler era; one that has gracefully made the transition to the 20th century. Perhaps Heaton Treadway said it best in 1930: "It seems to me that perhaps in all New England there is no town more typical of the existing times than is Stockbridge. An Indian village, the first white settlers coming as missionaries to it, the home of the most stringent orthodoxy, an active participant in the early literary development, the originator of civic pride organizations (The Laurel Hill Association — the oldest town beautification organization in the U.S.), a noted and increasingly popular summer and autumn resort — what could be more typical in New England life as portraying our country's development yesterday, today, and we hope, tomorrow? And almost from its settlement the public house stood on the corner of the main street...." — forever watching and participating in it all. Long Live The Red Lion Inn!

*And the long familiarity that makes folk feel at
  home.*

*The Treadways up in Stockbridge, at the old Red
  Lion sign,*
*Have an Inn that they've been running now for
  season eighty-nine.*
*Old friends will know that here's a place to spend a
  grand vacation,*
*New England hospitality is the best in all the
  nation.*
*Near symphony at Tanglewood, near Stockbridge
  Players too,*
*Not far from Ted Shawn's Dancers, all waiting here
  for you;*
*With the Berkshire Hills around you, far from
  urban heat and din,*
*Come and join us up in Stockbridge at the famed
  Red Lion Inn.*

*The Fitzpatricks have been running it, the old Red
  Lion Inn,*
*Its years are now two hundred; we hope you will
  come in.*
*Near skiing down at Butternut, near Norman
  Rockwell's paintings, too,*
*Not far from Bousquet skiing, all waiting here for
  you.*
*With the Berkshire Hills around you, far from
  urban crowd and din,*
*Come and join us up in Stockbridge at the famed
  Red Lion Inn."*

ABOUT NEW ENGLAND COOKING

When the Pilgrims first arrived in New England, they found seafood so plentiful that lobsters big enough to feed four people could be picked from rocky pools at low tide, abundant clams could be gathered from the sandy beaches, and eels and fish could be caught by the handfuls from the streams.

Francis Higginson, a Puritan minister in the Massachusetts Bay Colony, wrote home to England in 1629 that "the abundance of sea fish are almost beyond believing." He goes on to describe whale, sea bass, mackerel, skate, lobsters, herring, turbot, sturgeon, haddock, eels, crabs, mussels, oysters, and clams.

To take advantage of this abundance year-round, New Englanders became adept at salting and drying fish, especially codfish, and the fishing industry rapidly grew into one of utmost importance. By 1640, it had reached such proportions that in one year, New Englanders prepared 300,000 dried codfish for market.

Their success led to further enterprises. Producing more dried fish than England and America could consume, the colonists began to export it to the Mediterranean and the Caribbean, where there was a ready market. Rather than return with empty ships, however, the prudent captains filled their holds with molasses, a byproduct of the West Indies sugar refining business. In New England, molasses was used to make rum and eventually exported as well, along with pickled beef and pork.

Eventually, molasses became the preferred sweetener for the New England homemaker. It was used in baked beans, brown bread, gingerbread, Indian pudding, and wherever we might use sugar today. It probably served as a tasty counterpoint to all the salt pork and salt cod eaten. In fact, molasses played a role in the creation of the United States.

The American Revolution, was, after all, a rebellion based on taxes levied against New Englander's pocketbooks, and on their food — on such items as tea, molasses, and Madeira. John Adams once said, in reference to the Molasses Act passed by the British Parliament in 1733, "I know not why we should blush to confess that molasses is an essential ingredient in American independence."

The seeds for crops common in England, brought by the early settlers, proved difficult to grow, so it didn't take long for the Pilgrims to adapt their knowledge of food preparation to the Indian crops: corn, beans, and squash. It was that or live only on fish. Because the Pilgrims fled from a government they distrusted, they refused to seek help from England, even when threatened with starvation. This forced them to build a self-sustaining agricultural system in just one generation.

They learned to dry and pulverize corn, for example, and when they did, they found they could separate the finest granules to form a corn flour. It stubbornly remained coarse and crumbly when baked, however, refusing to rise as wheat and rye do. So the Pilgrim women made a thin batter with corn flour and water and poured it on a griddle. And that's how johnnycake, a delectable pancake loved by New Englanders, was born.

Benjamin Franklin was especially fond of johnnycakes. In 1766 he wrote in the *Gazetteer,* in reply to an Englishman who had said Indian corn was not "an agreeable...breakfast": "Pray, let me, an American, inform the gentleman, who seems ignorant of the matter, that Indian corn, take it for all in all, is one of the most agreeable and wholesome grains in the world...and that johnny or hoecake, hot from the fire, is better than a Yorkshire muffin."

The Pilgrims learned that if they boiled the corn with water, they had a nice mush for a hot breakfast treat, or to serve with meat at dinner. Roger Williams described hasty pudding in 1643 in *A Key into the Language of America* as "a kind of meale pottage, unpartch'd. From this the English call their Samp, which is the Indian corne, beaten, and boiled, and eaten hot or cold with milk or butter...and which is a dish exceeding wholesome for the English bodies."

Leftover corn mush (never let it be said a New England housewife wasted anything!) was formed into blocks, sliced and fried, and eaten with maple syrup or molasses.

Indian pudding, a concoction of corn meal and milk, eggs, sugar, butter, and cinnamon, was another popular treat. The Red Lion Inn recipe for Indian pudding is a very old one that has been served at the inn for well over a hundred years.

*"Fath'r and I went down to camp
Along with Captain Goodin,
And there we saw the men and boys
As thick as hasty puddin'."*

Yankee Doodle, 18th-century song

Indian pudding was not a dish the Indians invented, however. Rather, the name was devised to distinguish this yellow kernel from English corn, which we know as wheat. Thus, a dish made from Indian corn was called Indian pudding.

Beans were of utmost importance to the Pilgrims also, partly because they were plentiful, which made them cheap, and partly because they were so integral to the observation of the Sabbath. No work was allowed on the Sabbath, which extended from sundown Saturday to sundown Sunday — not even cooking. So the pot of beans went into the brick oven on Friday night, and emerged, in the form of piping-hot baked beans, in time for the Saturday night meal. Traditionally, this hearty feast was served with a brown bread, and the saying went "Brown bread and the Gospel is good fare." They were eaten for breakfast Sunday, and again on return from church Sunday afternoon. Every week this ritual was repeated. Later, baked beans became popular tavern fare. The Red Lion Inn's version is based on the earliest traditional recipes.

If Saturday was Baked Beans and Brown Bread day, Wednesday in New England was Boiled Dinner Day, just as Thursday was reserved for Corned Beef Hash, using the leftovers from Wednesday's meal. Friday's meal was fish — sometimes a hearty chowder, such as the version in Chapter 4.

Another of the earliest crops — and one that delighted the Pilgrims — was a bright red berry the Indians ate prodigiously. We know it today as the cranberry, and it continues to grow in abundance on Cape Cod. It's a traditional part of our Thanksgiving feasts, just as it was for the Pilgrims in 1621. Early sailors learned that cranberries were a good cure for scurvy and carried casks of them on their return voyages. John Josselyn, visiting New England in 1663, wrote: "The Indians and English use them much, boyling them with Sugar for Sauce to eat with their Meat, and it is a delicate sauce." The Red Lion Inn's version of cranberry sauce is found in Chapter 7.

Blackberries were another matter altogether. To the Pilgrims, blackberries were a pernicious nuisance, a weed only discussed when trying to figure out how to get rid of it. It crept into the early cookbooks, originally as a fruit for medicinal purposes. It wasn't until the 1830s that the weed was accepted as an edible fruit and gradually became popular.

Early settlers ate wild turkey and other fowl when they could shoot them, but meat was not plentiful, except when the Indians might shoot a deer for them. What a treat that was! Cattle were imported in 1624, but it took a number of years for them to multiply sufficiently to provide a steady source of

"She that is ignorant in cookery may love and obey, but she cannot cherish and keep her husband."

Seventeenth-century proverb

meat, milk, cheese, and butter. By 1650, however, the cattle had been joined by chickens, hogs, fruit from the seedling trees brought from England, vegetables in the garden, and rye and wheat. Now, the Pilgrim housewife had sufficient provisions to create a distinctive cuisine.

To that New England housewife, thrift and economy were the most important elements of cooking. Virtually nothing was wasted and inventive uses for leftovers abounded. Bones from a chicken or ham were re-used in soups and everything that wasn't used immediately was either pickled or salted.

To vary the numerous fish dishes early New Englanders were forced to eat, housewives devised a wide variety of sauces. A 1763 Boston cookbook, for example, suggests anchovies, pickled mushrooms, pickled walnuts, oysters, mussels, lobster, shrimp, lemon peel, vinegar, and every imaginable spice as additives to sauces.

Desserts in New England were quite another matter. The first settlers had no sugar (they eventually imported it from the West Indies) and seemed to like tart flavors at any rate, preferring to eat cranberries and berries without a sweetener. The Indians, however, had learned to score the bark of the mighty maple tree to obtain the sweet sap that ran in winter, and undoubtedly the Pilgrims copied them. A French Jesuit priest in 1671 wrote of "a liquor that runs from the trees toward the end of winter and is known as maple-water." The abundance and low cost of molasses made it the preferred sweetener, however.

Thrifty New England housewives elevated American pie to icon status. This combination of berries or fruit with a crust was not an American invention, but the colonists depended on and popularized the pie for its convenience and goodness. It was not unusual for a woman with a large family to make fifty, eighty, or even a hundred pies a week, setting them outside in the snow to freeze in winter and then placing them before the fireplace to thaw just before a meal.

Pies were eaten for breakfast, midday dinner, and supper — and especially popular was the apple pie. "As American as apple pie" is a saying that is based on historical fact. In 1758, a Swedish visitor by the name of Dr. Acrelius wrote home: "Apple pie is used through the whole year, and when fresh apples are no longer to be had, dried ones are used. It is the evening meal of children." But for one person at least, all that apple pie became tiresome, as this anonymous

President Coolidge, who visited The Red Lion Inn before and after becoming president, was once asked what was his greatest disappointment in the White House. He replied in typical New England fashion, and without the slightest hesitation, that it was his inability to find out what happened to the leftovers.

The First Ladies Cook Book

poem indicates:

"I loathe, abhor, detest, despise,
Abominate dried apple pies.
Tread on my corns and tell me lies,
But don't pass me dried apple pies."

Colonial cooking was an exercise in inventiveness. The iron pot, the most important utensil, was suspended on a pole made of green wood over the fire in the fireplace. The pole had to be checked frequently to be sure it hadn't burned through. If one forgot, the dinner might be unceremoniously dumped into the coals. How modern the housewife must have felt, when she replaced the stick of green wood with a forged iron rod fit on a ratchet that allowed the pot to be raised and lowered over the fire! The spider, a black iron frying pan with legs, which sat on the open hearth, was the precursor to today's iron skillet, still valued for its even spread of heat.

As New Englanders became more prosperous, they traveled more. By the late 18th century, tavern fare at wayside inns like The Red Lion Inn was simple but usually ample, centering around a meat dish or a stew, with boiled vegetables and a cornmeal bread. Large inns had much greater variety, but small inns generally made up for it in quantity.

An English traveler described the fare at the typical American tavern of 1807. "It is the custom in all American taverns, from the highest to the lowest, to have a sort of public table at which the inmates of the house and travellers dine together at a certain hour. It was also frequented by many single gentlemen belonging to the town...upwards of thirty sat down to dinner, though there were not more than a dozen who resided in the house.... At the better sort of American Taverns very excellent dinners are provided, consisting of almost everything in season. The hour is from two to three o'clock, and there are three meals in the day. They breakfast at eight o'clock upon rump steaks, fish, eggs, and a variety of cakes with tea or coffee. The last meal is at seven in the evening, and consists of as substantial fare as the breakfast, with the addition of cold fowl, ham, etc. ... Brandy, hollands, and other spirits are allowed at dinner, but every other liquor is paid for extra. English breakfasts and teas, generally speaking, are meager repasts compared with those of America, and as far as I observed the people live with respect to eating in a much more luxurious manner than we do."

A Red Lion Inn menu dating from 1922.

Stockbridge was charmingly described by another member of Stockbridge's Sedgwick family, Henry Dwight; he and his many cousins spent every summer at the family homestead. He relates: "The store [probably across the street from The Red Lion Inn] was a place to linger in, stare at cans, at bags of merchandise, ploughs, bridles, rope, candies under the glass case, all of which told stories of the wide and varied lands from which they came; and there you met your acquaintances, Mike Farley, a big, broad-shouldered, burly, smiling, jolly good fellow, and such.

"You bought dried hams at the store, but for fresh meat you welcomed Roger Barry, who came every day with his sorrel nag and his covered wagon."

The food served today at The Red Lion Inn is a reflection of New England's historic heritage. The stockpot is always brewing! Chef Steve Mongeon explains, "The Red Lion Inn menu is the billboard of traditional New England fare, but of the 1980s and 1990s — not two hundred years ago. We've adapted traditional New England recipes for today's healthy attitudes." And now, we welcome you to do the same.

APPETIZERS AND HORS D'OEUVRE

Generally, hors d'oeuvre are the finger foods that are served at a cocktail party or stand-up gathering before a dinner, and appetizers are the light first course at a sit-down dinner — but, or course, many dishes can be used both ways. In this chapter we present several recipes in each category — all popular selections at The Red Lion Inn.

First course appetizers have been popular starters for dinner parties for many years. Indeed, before Prohibition in 1920, entertaining was often on a lavish scale. Many-coursed dinner parties were waited on by legions of servants, where multiple appetizers were served before the entree. Some of these Berkshire dinner parties, hosted by Vanderbilts, Westinghouses, Stokeses, Fosters, and Sloanes, were said to be so elaborate that there might be up to ten courses and two or three servants per guest.

During the Depression, many Americans didn't have the time or the money to entertain on such a lavish scale. Thus, the cocktail party was devised — after Prohibition was over, of course, in 1933. It was a relatively inexpensive way to entertain a large gathering of friends.

Cocktail parties remain a popular way of entertaining today. The Red Lion Inn is noted for the parties it caters, from large corporate Christmas festivities in the dining room, to small intimate dinner parties in the Treadway Room, to wedding receptions in the courtyard. A popular summer cocktail food at The Red Lion Inn is a huge silver bowl filled with juicy fresh strawberries, served with powdered sugar. Another popular offering is a large bowl of fresh shrimp with a tangy cocktail sauce.

A basket of crudités is served at the table for Red Lion Inn guests to munch on while selecting their meal. For today's health-conscious party-goer, Chef Mongeon has devised a low calorie dip composed of yogurt and cottage cheese, which he serves at parties with a bowl of crispy fresh carrot sticks, celery, and green peppers.

Guests of The Red Lion Inn enjoy sitting in the lobby, especially in the winter, when a blazing fire takes the chill off cold noses. In summer, the preferred spot is the spacious porch, filled with comfortable wicker rocking chairs and armchairs. Both spots are pleasant places to sip a cocktail and snack on the crackers laid out on heaping platters on the sideboard, accompanied by a soft cheese.

"Our life is nothing but a winter's day;
Some only breakfast and away;
Others to dinner stay and are full fed.
The deepest age but sups and goes to bed.
He's worst in debt who lingers out the day.
Who goes betimes has all the less to pay."

Old Tavern Song

8 ounces thinly sliced smoked
   salmon (about 8 slices)

1 cup sour cream

8 teaspoons coarse prepared
   mustard

4 teaspoons finely chopped fresh
   dill

4 very thin slices red onion

4 teaspoons capers

thinly sliced pumpernickel bread

SMOKED SALMON RED LION

1. Arrange the slices of smoked salmon on serving plate.

2. Thoroughly mix the sour cream, mustard, and dill in a small bowl, and spoon over the salmon.

3. Garnish with the onion slices and capers.

4. Serve, with the pumpernickel bread in a basket alongside.

Serves 4.

ESCARGOTS RED LION

1. Bake the pastry shells as directed on the package, and keep warm.

2. Drain the liquid from the escargots. Place escargot butter, snails, and mushrooms in a sauté pan over medium heat and cook until the butter has melted, stirring occasionally.

3. Add the cream and 2 tablespoons of the parsley to the pan, stirring to mix thoroughly, simmer until the sauce has thickened slightly, stirring occasionally, about 20 minutes.

4. Spoon the snails and mushrooms into the pastry shells and pour the sauce over them. Garnish with remaining 2 tablespoons parsley.

Serves 4.

4 frozen puff pastry shells

1/2 cup Escargot Butter (recipe below)

28 canned escargots (snails)

8 to 10 fresh mushrooms, sliced

1 cup heavy cream

4 tablespoons parsley, chopped

ESCARGOT BUTTER

1. Combine all the ingredients in a bowl, and mix well. Store in an airtight container. This will keep for two to three days in refrigerator, or up to a week in the freezer.

Yields 1/2 cup.

1/2 cup butter, softened

2 teaspoons fresh garlic, minced

2 teaspoons onion, minced

2 teaspoons parsley, rinsed and chopped

2 teaspoons shallots, minced

1 teaspoon lemon juice

2 teaspoons garlic powder

pinch black pepper

pinch cayenne pepper

1 teaspoon white wine

1 pound small button mushrooms

1 medium onion

²/₃ cup cider vinegar

¹/₂ cup salad oil

1 clove garlic, minced

1 tablespoon sugar

1 ¹/₂ teaspoons salt

pepper to taste

2 tablespoons water

dash Tabasco sauce

MARINATED MUSHROOMS

This dish is sometimes served at The Red Lion Inn, along with fresh vegetables and olives, before the first course.

1. Wash the mushrooms and pat them dry, leaving them whole. Peel and thinly slice the onion into rounds. Place the mushrooms and onions in a plastic bowl with a cover, and set aside.

2. Mix the remaining ingredients together in a saucepan. Bring to a boil, stirring, to combine thoroughly. Remove the pan from the heat.

3. Place the mushrooms and onions in a plastic bowl with a cover. Pour the hot liquid over them, and marinate overnight in the refrigerator.

Serves 4.

A view of the front porch of The Red Lion Inn, 1894.

SCALLOPS AND BACON DIJON

When using bacon to wrap scallops or any other food, it is important to partially cook the bacon first, to eliminate some of the fat and water before broiling or roasting. This bite-size hors d'oeuvre is often top on the list of requests at Red Lion Inn cocktail parties.

1. Wash and clean the scallops. Pat dry.

2. Combine the wine, mustard, salt, and pepper in a bowl, and mix well. Add the scallops and toss to coat them with the mixture. Marinate, covered, in the refrigerator, for 1 hour.

3. Preheat the oven to 250°. Arrange the bacon slices in a single layer on a baking sheet and place in a 250° oven for 10 minutes, or until soft. Drain the bacon on paper towels, and cut each slice in half crosswise. Raise the oven heat to 350°.

4. Drain the scallops and wrap a bacon strip around each one, fastening it with a toothpick.

5. Arrange the scallops on a sheet pan and bake for 8 to 10 minutes, basting once with the juice they produce. Serve hot.

Serves 10.

20 sea scallops

2 tablespoons white wine

2 tablespoons Dijon mustard

$1/8$ teaspoon salt

pinch of pepper

10 strips of bacon

20 wooden toothpicks

$^1/_2$ pound fresh crabmeat, flaked

5 tablespoons butter

3 tablespoons onion, chopped

3 tablespoons flour

1 cup milk

$^1/_8$ teaspoons salt

pinch cayenne pepper

2 tablespoons Parmesan cheese, grated

2 tablespoons dried bread crumbs

1 tablespoon parsley, chopped

24 medium mushrooms, stems removed

2 tablespoons dry sherry

6 tablespoons Gruyère cheese, grated

Mushrooms Stuffed with Crabmeat and Gruyère

1. Preheat oven to 350°.

2. Carefully pick over the crabmeat to remove any cartilage and shell fragments.

3. Melt 3 tablespoons of the butter in a sauté pan. Add the onions and sauté over medium heat until translucent, about 3 minutes. Add the flour and cook an additional 3 minutes. Then add the milk and cook 5 to 6 minutes more, stirring, until thick and creamy. Do not let the mixture scorch. Remove from the heat.

4. Add the crabmeat, salt, cayenne pepper, and Parmesan cheese to the pan, and combine well. Stir in the bread crumbs and parsley. At this point the mixture should be as thick as a stuffing. Allow it to cool to room temperature.

5. Heat the remaining 2 tablespoons butter in another sauté pan, and sauté the mushroom caps until tender, about 3 minutes. While the pan is still hot, pour in the sherry and carefully light it with a match. Drain the caps and allow them to cool.

6. Mound 1 tablespoon of the stuffing in each mushroom cap, and sprinkle them with the Gruyère cheese.

7. Place caps on a greased baking sheet and bake at 350° for 10 minutes, until bubbling. Serve hot.

Serves 4 as an appetizer, and more as an hors d'oeuvre.

"The best thing about a cocktail party is being asked to it."

Gerald Nachman

PÂTÉ

1. Preheat the oven to 350°.

2. Pour Madeira or cognac into a skillet and cook over medium-high heat until reduced by half, about 5 minutes.

3. Melt the butter in another pan, and sauté the onions in it until they are translucent, about 3 minutes. Add the livers and cook until they are pink in the middle, about 10 minutes.

4. Grind the livers, onions, and meats in a food processor or a meat grinder, and transfer them to a large bowl. Add the eggs, spices, herbs and garlic, and combine thoroughly. Add the reduced Madeira or cognac, and blend it in.

5. Arrange the bacon strips across the width of a loaf pan, letting the ends extend over the sides of the pan. Place the ground mixture in the pan, filling it approximately three-fourths of the way. Pack it down well by tapping the pan on a hard surface. Fold the ends of the bacon strips over the top of the loaf, and arrange the bay leaves in a line down the center. Cover the pan with foil.

6. Place the loaf pan in a larger pan, and fill the larger pan with boiling water so that it reaches halfway up the sides of the loaf pan. Bake at 350° for approximately 1 1/2 hours. The pâté is done when it has shrunk slightly from the sides of the pan, there are no traces of rosy color, and the juices run clear.

7. Remove the foil, and drain off all the fat. Place a clean piece of foil on top of the pâté. Place the loaf pan in the refrigerator with another loaf pan set on top to press the pâté down. Fill the second pan with something heavy to weight it. Allow the pâté to chill for at least 24 hours before serving.

8. Serve by slicing into thin pieces with the bacon still in place.

Serves 18 to 20.

1/2 cup Madeira or cognac

2 tablespoons butter

1/2 cup onion, finely minced

2 cups duck, turkey, or chicken livers

1 1/4 cup pork, veal, or turkey meat, or combination of all, chopped

2 eggs, slightly beaten

1 1/2 teaspoons salt

1/2 teaspoons pepper

1 tablespoon ground allspice

3/4 teaspoon dried thyme

2 cloves garlic, mashed

1 tablespoon garlic powder

4 strips bacon, raw

4 whole bay leaves for garnish

2 whole chicken breasts, skinned and boned

2 eggs

2 teaspoons water

1 ¹/₂ cups macadamia nuts, finely chopped

³/₄ cup dried bread crumbs

³/₄ cup cornstarch

³/₄ cup clarified butter *(recipe follows)*

Cumberland Sauce *(recipe follows)*

CHICKEN MACADAMIA WITH CUMBERLAND SAUCE

The sauce for this delectable dish should be made 24 hours in advance.

1. Preheat the oven to 350°. Butter a baking sheet.

2. Cut the chicken breasts into long strips, about ¹/₄" wide, then cut each strip into pieces 1" long.

3. Combine the eggs and water in a shallow bowl, and mix well. In another shallow bowl, stir together the macadamia nuts and the bread crumbs. Prepare separate bowls for the clarified butter and the cornstarch.

4. Dip the chicken pieces in the coatings in this order: butter, cornstarch, egg mixture, and the nut mixture.

5. Arrange the chicken in a single layer on the prepared baking sheet, and cook for 12 to 15 minutes, or until golden brown. Serve on a tray with the Cumberland Sauce at room temperature, on the side.

Serves 4 to 6.

CLARIFIED BUTTER

1 pound butter

1. Dice the butter and place it in the top of a double boiler over very low heat, keeping the water warm but not hot. Let the butter melt gently. Do not stir. Remove from the heat. Allow to sit for 40 to 50 minutes, until the butter separates and the solids fall to the bottom. Gently pour the clear liquid on top through a piece of doubled cheesecloth (this will remove any remaining milk solids) into a bowl or jar.

NOTE: Excess clarified butter can be poured into a plastic dish with a lid, and stored in the refrigerator for several weeks, cutting off portions as needed. Clarified butter has a higher burning point than whole butter, and is ideal for sautéing or roasting delicate meats and fish, and in sauces.

Yields 1 cup.

CUMBERLAND SAUCE

$^1/_2$ cup port wine

1 cinnamon stick, about 3 inches long

2 whole cloves

1 orange

2 cups orange juice

$^1/_2$ cup red currant jelly

2 tablespoons cornstarch

2 tablespoons cold water

1. Combine the port, cinnamon stick, and cloves in a saucepan and bring to a boil. Simmer over medium high heat until the port is reduced by half, about 10 minutes. Set the pan aside.

2. Meanwhile, peel the orange, removing only the zest (no white pith). Place the orange zest in water to cover, bring to a boil, and simmer for 2 minutes. Drain, and mince.

3. Add the minced orange peel, orange juice, and currant jelly to the reduced port. Bring to a boil and simmer for 5 minutes.

4. Combine the cornstarch and water in a small bowl, then add it to the port mixture, stirring well. Bring to a boil and cook over medium heat, for about 5 minutes, until thick. Strain. Chill for 24 hours before serving.

Yields 2 cups.

1 loaf French bread, sliced

4 wedges Danish Brie (about 2 $^1/_2$ ounces)

$^1/_4$ cup blanched slivered almonds

$^1/_4$ cup butter

12 strawberries, washed and hulled

24 green seedless grapes

20 slices Red Delicious apple, unpeeled

4 teaspoons parsley, chopped

BAKED BRIE AND FRUIT WITH FRENCH BREAD

1. Preheat the oven to 375°.

2. Wrap the French bread in foil, and bake it in the oven, until hot, about 15 minutes.

3. Place one piece of the Brie on each of four ovenproof plates, and bake them in the same oven as the bread, until it is hot and bubbly, about 8 minutes. Remove from the oven and allow the plate to cool slightly.

4. Sauté the almonds in the butter in a small pan over medium heat until golden, about 3 minutes. Pour the almonds over the baked Bries, which are still on the ovenproof plates. Arrange the fruit and bread around the sides of the Brie and sprinkle the Brie with the parsley.

5. Serve the plates with small knives on the side, encouraging guests to spread the Brie on the French bread. The fruit is eaten as an accompaniment.

Serves 4.

ORIENTAL SHRIMP WITH SPICY EGG NOODLES

32 shrimp

Oriental Marinade *(recipe follows)*

1 medium carrot, peeled

1 medium red bell pepper

5 scallions

5 tablespoons olive oil

1 pound dry fettuccine egg noodles

1. Shell and clean the shrimp. Marinate the shrimp in ¹/₂ cup of the Oriental Marinade, covered, at room temperature, for 4 hours.

2. Cut the carrot in half lengthwise; then slice into very thin half-moons. Remove seeds and pulp from the red pepper and cut into thin julienne strips. Cut the tops off the scallions and slice them very thin on the diagonal.

3. Heat 4 tablespoons of the oil in a skillet, and sauté the carrot in the oil over high heat for 1 minute. Add the pepper and sauté for 3 additional minutes. Add the scallions and saute just until the scallion is bright green (about 1 minute), and remove from heat. Drain the vegetables, and set them in the refrigerator to cool.

4. Cook the noodles in salted water to cover, about 12 to 15 minutes until tender. Drain. Toss with the remaining 1 tablespoon olive oil to prevent sticking and cool to room temperature.

5. Drain the shrimp, reserving the marinade. Grill the shrimp over charcoal or on a grill until done and until the marinade is slightly caramelized, about 5 minutes.

6. Toss the noodles, vegetables and 1 ¹/₂ cups of the marinade together. Divide the mixture among eight plates, and arrange four shrimp on top of each serving. Sprinkle the reserved marinade over the shrimp in each serving. Serve the remaining marinade on the side. Serve at room temperature.

Serves 8.

2 tablespoons soy sauce

2 ¹/₂ tablespoons light brown sugar

¹/₂ tablespoon garlic, minced

¹/₄ cup + 2 tablespoons rice wine vinegar

¹/₂ tablespoon dried red pepper flakes

2 ¹/₄ cups corn oil

ORIENTAL MARINADE

1. Mix the soy sauce, brown sugar, garlic, vinegar, and red pepper flakes in a bowl, and stir until the sugar has dissolved.

2. Slowly add the corn oil, whisking briskly to emulsify.

Yields 3 cups.

6 sheets prepared frozen puff pastry, thawed to room temperature

¹/₄ cup butter, melted

¹/₂ cup Parmesan cheese, grated

1 teaspoon paprika

CHEESE STRAWS

1. Preheat the oven to 425°. Grease a sheet pan.

2. Roll each sheet of pastry out on a lightly floured board, until it is double in size (about 10" square). Brush with melted butter.

3. Combine the Parmesan cheese and paprika in a small bowl, and sprinkle about one-half on the buttered pastry, reserving the rest for the next step.

4. Fold each square in half and then roll it up to form a long cylinder. Sprinkle with more of the cheese mixture. Using two hands, roll the dough into a twist by rolling each hand gently in the opposite direction. Cut each cylinder into thirds (each about 3 ¹/₂" long), and sprinkle with additional cheese mixture. Place the twists on the prepared sheet pan.

5. Bake at 425° for 10 minutes, until golden brown. Serve hot.

Yields 18 to 20 cheese straws.

HOT TENDERLOIN CANAPÉS ON PUMPERNICKEL WITH BLUE CHEESE

1. Butter a baking sheet.

2. Trim the tenderloin steak of all fat and tissue. Brush with the Italian Dressing, cover, and allow to marinate in the refrigerator for 2 hours.

3. Combine the cheeses, Worcestershire sauce, and horseradish in a bowl, and mix thoroughly. Cover and chill for 1 hour.

4. Preheat the oven to 350°. Char-grill or pan fry the tenderloin until rare, about 6 minutes on the first side and 5 minutes on the second. Cool.

5. Cut rounds about 1" diameter in size from the slices of bread. (You should be able to get four rounds from each slice, for a total of 40 rounds.) Brush the bread rounds on both sides with the melted butter. Bake them at 350° on the prepared baking sheet, turning them over once, until crisp, about 8 to 10 minutes. Remove them from the oven and preheat the broiler.

6. Leaving the bread rounds on the baking sheet, lightly spread them with some of the cheese mixture. Cut the cooled tenderloin into 40 very thin slices. Trim them as necessary to fit the bread rounds and place a slice on each round. Top each with a dab of cheese mixture, and arrange two pimiento strips, crossing them, on each tenderloin.

7. Broil the canapés until bubbly hot, 2 to 3 minutes. Serve immediately.

Yields 40 canapés.

$^1/_2$ pound tenderloin of beef

$^1/_4$ cup Robust Italian Dressing *(see page 53)*

$^1/_4$ cup cream cheese, softened

$^1/_4$ cup blue cheese, softened

$^1/_8$ teaspoon Worcestershire sauce

1 tablespoon prepared horseradish, drained

10 slices thin pumpernickel bread

$^1/_4$ cup butter, melted

80 very thin strips of pimiento

SOUPS AND STOCKS

The colonists, long familiar with French and English stews and soups, adapted the fish found in New England to their old recipes, adding spices, herbs, and other ingredients brought from the old country. Fresh seafood was readily available: eel, cod, oysters, clams, and lobsters were so plentiful they were thrown into the pot in prodigious quantities. Early cookbooks call for two hundred oysters for oyster stew, two quarts of clams for clam chowder, and eight lobsters for lobster stew.

Lobsters were so abundant that the colonists considered it an embarrassment to serve them to company. One early account describes a storm at Plymouth that left lobsters piled two feet high on the beach. They were so plentiful and so easily gathered that they were considered fit only for the poor, who could afford nothing better, and thus were used freely in everyday soups and stews.

Even clams, the staple of that most renowned of New England chowders, may have had an unpopular genesis. One report from the 1620s claims that Pilgrims fed clams and mussels to their hogs, as they were "the meanest of God's blessings." They may have been considered unfit for human consumption, but clams were abundant and could be disguised in a soup.

New England soups were born of practicality and economy. Thrifty tavern owners, such as those at The Red Lion Inn, reflected that practicality by serving hearty brews that simmered on the back of the tavern stove throughout the day, ready to warm the cold, weary traveler.

The Red Lion Inn continues to carry on the tradition of comfort inherited from stagecoach days. Here are a few of the many soups served at the inn.

Referring to stagecoach travel: "Psychology suggests that there is no pleasure greater than the relief from pain, and the arrival at one's destination must have been a delight in proportion to the discomforts undergone."

Old Inns of Connecticut

NEW ENGLAND CLAM CHOWDER

Chowders are so timelessly bound to New England cooking that we tend to assume they originated here, but they are probably adaptations of the stews and hearty soups made in England and France. The name seems to have come from the pot, called a "chaudiere," brought by Breton fisherman to Nova Scotia, where it eventually found its way down the coast to New England. It was customary for thrifty women to toss whatever edibles they had into the pot and cook it all together until tender.

Any good New England cook has his or her favorite recipe, but most will agree that a traditional chowder must include two ingredients — clams and salt pork — with a cream and stock base, just as this traditional old Red Lion Inn recipe does, and never tomatoes. In this delicious and easy-to-prepare version of the classic, The Red Lion Inn now substitutes margarine for the salt pork, to reduce the calorie content, although we have retained the original here.

1. In a large pot, combine the warm water, clams, and seasonings. Bring to a boil, and boil until the clams open, about 12 to 18 minutes. Discard any clams that do not open.

2. Strain the clams and reserve both clams and stock. Remove the meat from the clam shells and mince the clams. (If you are using canned minced clams, add them to the water and boil them 10 minutes. Strain and reserve the clams and the stock.)

3. Combine the potatoes and half of the clam stock in a large pot. Gently simmer until cooked but still firm, about 10 minutes. Drain, reserving the stock.

4. Place salt pork in a heavy soup pot, and sauté until partially rendered, about 5 minutes. Beware, as this will splatter. (Or, melt margarine in a heavy soup pot.)

5. Remove the pork from the pan and set it aside. Remove half of the melted fat. Sauté the onions in the remaining fat or margarine over medium heat until translucent but not brown, about 5 minutes.

4 cups warm water

2 dozen fresh clams in the shell (or 2 small cans minced clams)

1 teaspoon salt

$1/4$ teaspoon white pepper

$1/4$ teaspoon Worcestershire sauce

2 cups potatoes, peeled and diced

$1/4$ pound salt pork, diced, or $1/2$ cup margarine

1 cup onions, chopped

2 tablespoons flour

3 cups milk, scalded

1 cup light cream

2 tablespoons butter

6. Add the flour to the onions, and blend thoroughly to make roux. Cook over medium heat, stirring, for 5 to 6 minutes. (If you prefer a thicker chowder, more flour may be added at this point.)

7. Add all the reserved stock to the roux and stir until hot and smooth. Add the potatoes, clams, salt pork, scalded milk, and cream. Heat thoroughly but do not boil. Adjust seasonings and add the 2 tablespoons butter just before serving, stirring until it has melted.

Serves 10.

"Hot soup at table is very vulgar; it either leads to an unseemly mode of taking it, or keeps people waiting too long whilst it cools. Soup should be brought to table only moderately warm."

Hints on Etiquette, 1844

AUTUMN BISQUE SOUP

Every fall, the Berkshire Botanical Garden holds a Harvest Festival on its grounds in Stockbridge, and The Red Lion Inn provides a large pot of this Autumn Bisque to warm the throngs of hungry people. This heady concoction owes its distinctive flavor to butternut squash and tart apples. The recipe was highlighted in *Gourmet* magazine in September 1980, and remains just as popular today.

1. Combine the stock, onion, bread cubes, apples, squash, salt, marjoram, rosemary, and pepper in a large kettle. Bring to a boil over moderate heat and simmer for 45 minutes. Remove the squash with a slotted spoon and scoop out the flesh, returning the flesh to the soup and discarding the skin.

2. Puree the soup, in batches, in a blender. Return the puree to the rinsed-out kettle.

3. In a small bowl, beat together the egg yolks and cream. Stir a little soup into the egg mixture, and then stir this back into the soup.

4. Heat the soup over moderate heat until it is hot, but do not let it boil. Ladle the bisque into heated bowls, and serve.

Serves 4 to 6.

4 cups chicken stock *(see page 38)* or broth

1 cup onion, chopped

2 slices bread, crusts removed, cubed

2 tart apples, peeled, cored, and chopped coarse

1 pound butternut squash, halved lengthwise and seeded

1 1/2 teaspoons salt

1/4 teaspoon dried marjoram

1/4 teaspoon dried rosemary

1/4 teaspoon pepper

2 large egg yolks

1/4 cup heavy cream

3 tablespoons butter

¹/₃ cup leeks, diced

¹/₃ cup onion, diced

¹/₃ cup celery, diced

1 cup broccoli, diced

3 tablespoons flour

3 cups chicken stock *(see page 38)* or broth

salt, pepper to taste

dried thyme to taste

¹/₃ cup white wine

1 cup light cream

CREAM OF BROCCOLI SOUP

The Red Lion Inn's cream soups are popular in summer and winter. For variation, any vegetable — such as zucchini, carrots, spinach, asparagus, mushrooms, Brussels sprouts — may be substituted for the broccoli.

1. Melt the butter in a large saucepan and add the leeks, onion, celery, and broccoli. Saute about 5 minutes over low heat (do not allow the butter to brown).

2. Blend in the flour, and cook, stirring for 1 minute; then add the chicken stock. Bring to a boil. Add the salt, pepper, thyme, and wine. Let simmer until the vegetables are tender, about 20 minutes.

3. Remove the soup from the stove and puree it, in batches, in a blender. Return the puree to a saucepan over low heat and add the cream just before serving, stirring until heated through.

Serves 4.

STOCKBRIDGE LIBRARY ASSOCIATION HISTORICAL ROOM

The Red Lion Inn and Main Street in Stockbridge in 1890.

CREAM OF TOMATO AND CHEDDAR SOUP

In 1971 Jack Fitzpatrick organized the first Red Lion Inn Pro-Am Golf Tournament at the historic Stockbridge Golf Club. The tournament heralds autumn each September, and as the leaves ringing the course turn their red and golden hues, there's often a bite to the air. Chef Steve Mongeon has created this hearty soup to warm the weary golfers and it's now known as the official soup of The Red Lion Inn Golf Tournament.

1. Finely chop the onions, celery, and carrots. Heat the olive oil in a 4-quart soup pot, and sauté the vegetables over medium heat until slightly softened, about 5 minutes.

2. Add the tomatoes, including the juices, the bag of spices, Worcestershire sauce, Tabasco, and 2 cups of the veal or chicken stock. Bring to a boil, and simmer for 1 hour, stirring often.

3. Remove the spice bag (set it aside) and puree the mixture in small batches in a blender, until smooth.

4. Return the puree to the rinsed-out pot, add the remaining 6 cups veal or chicken stock and return the spice bag to the soup. Bring to a boil, reduce the heat, and simmer for about 45 minutes, until thickened.

5. Melt the ²/₃ cup of butter in a small saucepan and then stir in the flour. Cook over low heat for 5 minutes, creating a roux, but do not brown. Add the roux to the soup by spoonful, beating well after each addition. Bring to a boil and simmer for 10 minutes.

6. Add the cheddar cheese, remaining 1 cup butter (optional: this will create a very rich soup) and cream. Heat the soup but do not boil, as it will curdle. Adjust the seasonings, garnish with croutons, additional cheese, and chopped parsley, if desired, and serve immediately.

1 small onion, peeled

4 stalks celery, leaves removed

3 carrots, peeled

4 tablespoons extra virgin olive oil

2 pounds canned chopped Italian plum tomatoes

3 teaspoons whole mixed pickling spices, tied in a cheesecloth bag

2 teaspoons Worcestershire sauce

¹/₄ teaspoon Tabasco sauce

8 cups veal stock, or substitute chicken stock (see page 38)

²/₃ cup butter

²/₃ cup flour

³/₄ pound Vermont cheddar cheese, double aged (4 years) if possible, shredded

1 cup additional butter (optional)

1 cup heavy cream

Salt and pepper to taste

Garnish (optional): croutons, additional cheddar cheese, and chopped parsley

Serves 10.

6 medium sized onions

2 tablespoons olive oil

1 tablespoon garlic powder

1 cup red burgundy

$^1/_2$ cup sherry

$^3/_4$ cup Marsala

1 tablespoon dried thyme

1 tablespoon black peppercorns

1 tablespoon dried rosemary

1 square cheesecloth (about 6" x 6")

salt to taste

4 cups chicken stock *(see page 38)* or broth

4 cups beef stock *(see page 37)* or broth

One $^1/_4$" thick slice French bread per portion

$^1/_4$ cup butter, melted

$^1/_2$ cup Parmesan cheese, grated

dash paprika

BAKED ONION SOUP

This rich, hearty onion soup is a perennial favorite on the Red Lion Inn menu. Try it yourself and you'll see why.

1. Peel the onions and slice them into thin rings. Heat the oil in a soup pot, and add the onions and garlic powder. Sauté over low heat until tender and lightly caramelized, about 30 minutes.

2. Add the wines to the onions, and boil until reduced by a half, about 15 minutes.

3. Place the thyme, peppercorns, and rosemary in a cheesecloth square and tie the corners securely to form a bag.

4. Add the stocks and herb bag to the soup pot. Cook for approximately 1 hour over medium heat.

5. Preheat the oven to 375°.

6. Brush the bread slices with the melted butter on one side only. Sprinkle 1 teaspoon of the cheese on each slice, and top with a dash of paprika. Place the slices on a baking sheet, buttered side up, and bake in a 375° oven for 8 minutes. Remove the sheet from the oven, and preheat the broiler.

7. Pour the soup into individual ovenproof crocks, and top each serving with a slice of prepared bread. Sprinkle with the remaining cheese. Broil just until the cheese is bubbly, lightly browned, and crusted on top. Serve immediately.

Serves 10 to 12.

BEEF STOCK

A good stock is the basis for so many soups, sauces, and meat dishes, that a well-equipped kitchen will always have at least chicken and beef stocks on hand. For the thrifty New Englander, a stock was the final dish prepared after roasting beef, chicken, or turkey. Chef Mongeon prepares all his own stocks for the Red Lion Inn kitchen — including a duck stock, a turkey stock, a veal stock, a shrimp stock, and an au jus, in addition to the chicken and beef stocks we share here. If time is limited, excellent canned beef and chicken stocks are available at most grocery stores.

1. Preheat the oven to 350°.

2. Place the bones in a roasting pan in a 350° oven and roast until golden brown, 35 minutes to 1 hour.

3. Add the vegetables, garlic, and shallots to the roasting pot and roast until golden brown, approximately 1/2 hour more.

4. Transfer the bones and vegetables to a deep soup pot. Add the seasonings and enough water to cover by 1/2". Bring to a boil over high heat. Reduce the heat and simmer 1 1/2 hours.

5. Strain the stock, and skim the fat off the top. Allow it to cool in the refrigerator and remove additional fat that will form on the top. Store the stock in a glass or stainless steel container. It will keep in the refrigerator for up to 3 weeks, and freezes very well.

Yields 4 quarts.

5 pounds beef bones

2 carrots, peeled and sliced

6 stalks celery, cut into 1/2" pieces

1 medium onion, peeled and sliced

2 heads garlic, unpeeled and split in half

3 shallots, unpeeled and split in half

1 tomato, chopped

1 tablespoon thyme

1 tablespoon pepper

4 bay leaves

water to cover by 1/2"

5 pounds chicken bones

1 onion, peeled and sliced

2 carrots, peeled and cut into pieces

4 stalks celery, cut into pieces

2 heads garlic, unpeeled and split

3 shallots, unpeeled and split

1 tablespoon dried rosemary

4 bay leaves

1 tablespoon black peppercorns

1 tablespoon dried thyme

water to cover by $^1/_2$"

CHICKEN STOCK

1. Place all ingredients in a stockpot, add enough water to cover by $^1/_2$", and bring to a boil. Reduce the heat and simmer for 1 $^1/_2$ hours.

2. Strain the stock, and skim the fat off the top. Allow it to cool in the refrigerator and remove additional fat that will form on the top. Store the stock in a glass or stainless steel container. It will keep in the refrigerator for up to 3 weeks, and freezes very well.

Yields 4 quarts.

Chef Steve Mongeon carries on the New Englander's penchant for economy and frugality. He explains, "At home we always roast a chicken for Sunday dinner. That gives us enough leftover meat for delicious chicken salad sandwiches for the children's lunches. I throw the bones in a pot with fresh vegetables to make a stock, which I then freeze in cubes in ice trays. Then, when I make rice or pasta, I toss in a few cubes of stock for flavor."

ALPINE CHEESE SOUP

1. Brown the bacon lightly in a soup pot. Add the onion, celery, and scallions, and cook over low heat until soft, about 8 to 10 minutes.

2. Add the chicken broth, oats, salt, and pepper. Bring to a boil, then reduce heat and simmer slowly, for 40 minutes, uncovered. Watch the soup, as it boils over easily.

3. Puree the soup in batches in a blender and return it to the heat.

4. Beat the grated cheese into the soup and then add cream. Simmer until hot, but do not boil. Garnish with the parsley, and serve.

Serves 4 to 6.

4 slices lean bacon, chopped

$^1/_2$ medium onion, chopped

1 stalk celery, chopped

3 scallions, including tops, chopped

5 cups chicken broth *(see page 38)*

$^1/_2$ cup rolled oats

1 teaspoon salt

pepper to taste

$^1/_2$ cup Swiss cheese, grated

$^1/_4$ cup heavy cream

1 tablespoon parsley, chopped

1 pound dried green split peas

2 ¹/₂ quarts warm water

2 tablespoons bacon or pork fat

¹/₂ cup onion, diced small

¹/₂ cup carrots, peeled, diced small

¹/₂ cup celery hearts and leaves, diced small

¹/₂ teaspoon garlic powder

¹/₄ teaspoon dried thyme

1 teaspoon Worcestershire sauce

¹/₈ teaspoon Tabasco sauce

2 bay leaves

2 whole cloves

3 black peppercorns

2 pounds ham hocks or 1 meaty ham bone

1 pound potatoes, peeled and diced (optional)

salt and freshly ground pepper to taste

homemade croutons (*recipe follows*), bacon bits, and chopped parsley for garnish

OLD-FASHIONED SPLIT PEA SOUP WITH HAM

This thrifty peasant-style soup is excellent as a meal by itself, perhaps served with a crusty French bread, a salad, and a chilled bottle of Beaujolais.

1. Rinse the split peas in a strainer and remove any impurities. Soak them in the warm water for 6 to 8 hours or overnight.

2. Melt the fat in a large soup pot. When it is hot, add the onions, carrots, celery, garlic powder, thyme, Worcestershire, and Tabasco. Sauté over medium heat for 3 to 5 minutes, or until the vegetables are cooked, but still firm.

3. Place the bay leaves, cloves, and peppercorns on a cheesecloth square, and tie it up to form a small bag.

4. Add the split peas along with their soaking liquid, the ham hocks, and the bag of spices to the vegetables and bring to a boil. Skim off any foam that appears on the surface. Reduce the heat and simmer gently for 1 ¹/₂ hours, or simmer for 2 hours if not adding potatoes.

5. (Optional step) Add the diced potatoes, if desired, and simmer an additional 30 minutes.

6. Remove the ham hocks (or bone), and allow to cool slightly. Remove the fat, sinew, and gristle from the ham and chop the meat into small cubes.

7. Check the consistency of the soup. Add water if it is too thick. If it is too thin, continue to simmer until it has thickened to your liking. Add the diced ham. Taste for flavor and adjust seasonings to taste.

8. Ladle the soup into individual bowls and garnish with croutons, bacon bits, and chopped parsley sprinkled on the top.

Serves 8 to 10.

HOMEMADE CROUTONS

The Red Lion Inn uses these croutons as a garnishment to salads as well as soups.

1. Preheat the oven to 350°.

2. Cut the bread into ¹/₂" cubes and spread them on a large sheet pan.

3. Combine the spices in a small bowl and sprinkle them over the bread cubes.

4. Ladle the clarified butter over the bread cubes and bake at 350° for 15 minutes. Stir the croutons and continue baking and turning until croutons are golden brown on all sides. Watch, however, as they will burn easily.

5. Store the croutons in an airtight covered container until used. These will keep about 1 week.

Yields 5 cups.

5 slices day old bread or dinner rolls

¹/₂ teaspoon garlic salt

¹/₂ teaspoon ground basil

¹/₂ teaspoon ground oregano

¹/₂ cup clarified butter, melted *(see page 25)*

The Red Lion Inn at Christmas is homey and festive.

4 cups chicken stock (*see page 38*) or broth

1 small butternut squash (about 1 pound), peeled, seeded, and coarsely chopped

2 tart green apples, peeled and coarsely chopped

1 medium onion, coarsely chopped

1 small yellow turnip (about 4 ounces) peeled and chopped

1 1/2 teaspoons salt

1/4 teaspoon freshly ground pepper

pinch dried rosemary

2 large egg yolks

1/4 cup heavy cream

2 tablespoons sherry

CREAM OF APPLE AND TURNIP SOUP WITH SHERRY

This popular recipe has been winning rave reviews at The Red Lion Inn for years — so much so that it was printed in *Bon Appetit* magazine in December 1977.

1. Combine the stock, squash, apples, onion, turnip, and seasonings in a 4-quart saucepan and bring to a boil over high heat. Cover, and simmer until the vegetables are soft, about 45 minutes.

2. Remove from heat and allow the soup to cool slightly, about 10 minutes. Puree the soup, in batches, in a blender; return the soup to a rinsed-out saucepan.

3. Using a whisk, beat the yolks and cream together in a small bowl.

4. Gradually add about 1 cup of the puree to the egg mixture, stirring it in thoroughly. Stir this back into the remaining soup. Add the sherry and reheat but do not boil. Pour into soup bowls and serve immediately.

Serves 6.

COLD STRAWBERRY SOUP

This recipe is a favorite at The Red Lion Inn throughout the summer months.

1. Combine the strawberries, cinnamon, salt, orange juice, water, wine, and cloves in a saucepan, and bring to a boil over medium heat. Reduce the heat and simmer for 10 to 12 minutes.

2. Mix the cornstarch and water together in a small bowl. Stir $1/4$ cup of the strawberry mixture into the cornstarch and then add this back to the mixture on the stove. Bring to a boil and stir until thickened, about 5 minutes.

3. Let the mixture sit until cool, and then add the ice cream and light cream. Stir until the ice cream has melted. Refrigerate for 1 hour. Garnish each serving with a fresh strawberry.

Serves 6 to 8.

3 cups frozen strawberries

$1/4$ teaspoon ground cinnamon

$1/4$ teaspoon salt

4 ounces frozen orange juice concentrate

$1/2$ cup water

$1/4$ cup red burgundy wine

pinch ground cloves

1 $1/2$ tablespoons cornstarch

1 $1/2$ tablespoons water

1 pint vanilla ice cream

2 cups light cream

6 to 8 fresh whole strawberries, for garnish

2 medium onions, peeled and
chopped

4 stalks celery, chopped

3 carrots, peeled and chopped

1 cup plus 2 tablespoons butter

1 cup flour

2 quarts chicken stock *(see page 38)*
or broth

1 pound chicken breasts, boned
and skinned

$1/2$ cup white rice

1 teaspoon Worcestershire sauce

3 drops Tabasco sauce

salt and pepper to taste

$1/3$ cup plus 2 tablespoons dry
sherry

1 cup light cream

CREAM OF CHICKEN SOUP

1. Grind the onions, celery, and carrots in a food grinder fitted with a coarse blade, or in a food processor. Melt 1 cup of the butter in a deep pot. Add the vegetables and sauté for 3 minutes, over medium heat until opaque. Reduce the heat and add the flour. Cook, stirring constantly, for 10 minutes.

2. Slowly add the stock, whisking until smooth.

3. Bring the soup to a boil, add the chicken breasts, and reduce the heat to medium. Simmer gently, covered, for 20 to 30 minutes. Remove the chicken breasts from the pot and allow them to cool slightly, until able to handle. Finely dice the chicken, and return it to the soup. Add the rice, seasonings, and $1/3$ cup of the sherry. Simmer gently for 1 hour or until rice disintegrates.

4. Add the light cream and stir until hot, but do not boil. Stir in the remaining 2 tablespoons butter and 2 tablespoons sherry, taste for seasoning, and serve.

Serves 8 to 10.

"Aunt Mert approved original design for sign but Uncle Charles opposed on the grounds that the lion was too thin and might reflect on his table."

Notation in the Red Lion Inn's guest book, May 1936

Salads and Salad Dressings

Salads of lettuce and other greens were popular in Europe, especially in France, in the seventeenth century, but their popularity was not generally transported to America. The earliest salads in this country favored sliced cucumbers and onions, marinated in vinegar — actually, cucumbers on their way to becoming pickles. Coleslaw, shredded cabbage with a dressing, was introduced by the Dutch and also became an early American favorite.

Thomas Jefferson, who had become a dedicated Francophile when he was an envoy to France, loved the fresh, green salads served in that country as palate cleansers immediately after the main course. He carefully planned his garden to have an abundance of fresh greens available throughout the summer — it is said that he had up to nineteen varieties of lettuce alone. But despite Jefferson's influence, James Beard tells us that green salads did not reach popularity in America until the late nineteenth century. And despite Jefferson's preference, Americans still eat their salads before the main course — a custom that is followed at The Red Lion Inn.

Sweet gelatin salads became popular in 1905, when a Pennsylvania housewife won a national cooking prize for hers. Although these molded salads are not as popular today as they once were, they add a refreshing variation to green salads, and are especially nice for special occasion dinners, such as Thanksgiving and Christmas.

The Red Lion Inn offers a wide variety of salads from traditional coleslaw to a grilled salmon and orange salad. In keeping with today's heightened consciousness about calorie and cholesterol intake, Chef Mongeon has developed a delicious low calorie dressing of water, vinegar, apple juice, and spices. "Every gram of fat," he explains, "contains 9 calories. That means that 1 teaspoon of dressing with an oil base will contain at least 120 calories. One teaspoon of the low calorie dressing, however, contains under 10 calories."

"A salad is a sort of mealtime magician, able to jump in and supply the contrasts that make meals sparkle."

The General Foods Cookbook

6 whole chicken breasts

1 quart chicken stock *(see page 38)*

1 cup chicken salad dressing *(recipe below)*

1 large white onion, shredded

$^1/_2$ cup carrots, shredded

3 cups shredded white cabbage

$^1/_3$ cup unsalted pistachio nuts

salt and pepper to taste

1 pineapple, skinned, cored, and cubed

tomato wedges, for garnish

black olives, for garnish

$^1/_2$ cup rice vinegar

1 $^3/_4$ cup corn oil

3 tablespoons sugar

$^3/_4$ teaspoon Worcestershire sauce

pinch white pepper

$^3/_4$ teaspoon salt

RED LION INN CHICKEN SALAD

This recipe is a special favorite of owner Jane Fitzpatrick. It's a refreshing summer salad that's especially enjoyed outdoors under the shade of the trees in the courtyard.

1. Bring the chicken stock to a boil, add the chicken breasts, and reduce the heat to medium. Simmer gently, covered, for 20 to 30 minutes. Remove the chicken breasts from the pot and allow them to cool slightly, until able to handle. Remove the meat from the bones. Discard the skin and fat; you may wish to freeze the bones for use in a chicken stock later. Julienne the meat of the chicken breasts.

2. Combine the dressing, onion, carrots, cabbage, and chicken in a large bowl. Marinate, covered, for a minimum of 1 hour, 3 to 4 hours if possible.

3. Just before serving, toss the pistachio nuts into the salad, reserving a few for garnish. Season with salt and pepper. Pile on individual plates and garnish with the pineapple, remaining nuts, tomato wedges, and olives.

Serves 6.

CHICKEN SALAD DRESSING

1. Combine all ingredients in a jar or a bowl, and shake or whisk well.

Yields 2 $^1/_2$ cups.

Duck Salad with Strawberry Vinaigrette

This is one of the Red Lion Inn's most popular summer salads, and a marvelous way to use up extra strawberries, should you have a bountiful garden crop.

1. Skin and bone the ducks. Place the duck meat in a large bowl, add 4 cups of the Strawberry Vinaigrette, and marinate, covered, for 1 hour.

2. Char-grill or quickly sauté the duck meat over medium heat until medium rare. Slice the duck meat diagonally across the grain into julienne strips.

3. Divide the torn lettuce among 4 plates. Top the lettuce with the spinach. Sprinkle the strawberries and mushrooms over the greens. Arrange the orange and apple slices, alternating, around the edge of the plate. Place the strips of duck over the berries and mushrooms; top with the onion rings.

4. Serve the salad, passing the remaining Strawberry Vinaigrette on the side.

Serves 4.

2 whole ducks

5 cups Strawberry Vinaigrette *(recipe below)*

1 cup red or green leaf lettuce leaves, torn

1 cup spinach leaves, washed and torn

1 cup strawberries, sliced

1 cup mushrooms, sliced

12 orange sections

12 apple slices, cored, but not peeled

8 rings red onion, thinly sliced

Strawberry Vinaigrette

1. Puree the fresh and frozen strawberries together in a blender or food processor until smooth.

2. Add the vinegar, and then slowly add the oil while the blender is running. Blend until the dressing is thoroughly emulsified.

3. Mix in the spices by hand.

Yields 7 cups.

$^{1}/_{2}$ pint fresh strawberries

2 cups sweetened frozen strawberries, thawed and drained

$^{1}/_{2}$ cup balsamic vinegar

4 cups olive oil

1 teaspoon dried thyme

1 tablespoon dried marjoram

4 cups red or green leaf lettuce,
    shredded

8 cups spinach leaves, washed
    thoroughly and torn

2 cups radicchio leaves, shredded

3/4 pound smoked chicken, cut in
    small pieces

3/4 pound extra sharp cheddar
    cheese, sliced 1/4" thick

12 slices of apple, cored but not
    peeled

12 wedges of tomato

1/2 cup Warm Chutney Dressing
    (recipe below)

3/4 cup prepared chutney

1 1/4 cup corn oil

2 tablespoons bacon fat

1/4 cup cider vinegar

1 tablespoon light brown sugar

2 tablespoons bacon, crisply
    cooked and chopped

SMOKED CHICKEN SALAD

1. Divide the shredded lettuce among four plates, piling it in the center of
   each. Pile the spinach on top of the lettuce, fluffing higher, if necessary, to
   create a mound.

2. Sprinkle the radicchio over the spinach, and then arrange the chicken in the
   center of the greens. Fan the cheese slices around the chicken. Arrange the
   apple and tomato wedges, alternating, around the edge of the plate.

3. Pour the Warm Chutney Dressing over all, and serve immediately.

Serves 4.

WARM CHUTNEY DRESSING

1. Combine all ingredients in a saucepan and heat over medium heat. Cook,
   stirring, until thoroughly blended and heated.

Yields 2 cups.

SPINACH AND BACON SALAD WITH WARM CHUTNEY DRESSING

4 Red Delicious apples, cored but not peeled

8 cups spinach, washed thoroughly and torn

2 cups mushrooms, sliced

8 thin slices red onion

1/2 cup Warm Chutney Dressing *(see page 48)*

12 slices bacon, fried crisp and crumbled

1. Place one fourth of the apple slices on each of four salad plates. Pile the spinach on top of the apples, and garnish with the mushrooms and onion.

2. Spoon the dressing over the spinach, and scatter the bacon on top. Serve immediately.

Serves 4.

"Though it seems a simple thing to prepare, a fine salad is an art. The greens must be fresh, crisp, and cool. They should not sport a drop of moisture when they are placed in a bowl. They should be broken into bite-size pieces or left in large pieces to be cut at table.... The perfect dressing should be neither oily nor acid. Sugar has no place in the dressing.... According to my experience, you should plan on a minimum of 2 cups of loosely packed greens per person...."

James Beard, American Cookery

2 Red Delicious apples

24 seedless red grapes

24 seedless green grapes

2 oranges, separated into sections

4 stalks celery

$^1/_2$ cup heavy cream

$^1/_2$ cup mayonnaise

2 teaspoons honey

pinch white pepper

8 lettuce leaves

2 bananas, sliced

$^1/_2$ cup walnuts, chopped

RED LION INN WALDORF-STYLE SALAD

The original Waldorf salad was created by Oscar Tschirky, maitre d' of the Waldorf-Astoria Hotel in New York, and was composed of apples and celery only. The Red Lion Inn version includes oranges, grapes, and bananas for added interest.

1. Core the apples, leaving skins on, and cut them into small cubes. Cut each of the grapes into quarters. Cut each of the orange sections into 5 to 6 smaller pieces.

2. Whip the cream in a bowl, until soft peaks form. Gently fold in the mayonnaise, and season with the honey and white pepper. Fold in the chopped fruit.

3. Arrange two lettuce leaves on each plate, and spoon the fruit salad in a mound in the center. Ring the plates with the banana slices, and sprinkle the walnuts over the fruit. Serve immediately.

Serves 4.

RED LION INN POTATO SALAD

Sometimes, as a sassy variation, Chef Mongeon will substitute his Robust Italian Dressing *(see page 53)* for the Ranch Dressing in this salad.

1 pound red-skinned potatoes, with the skins left on

$^1/_4$ cup celery, chopped

$^1/_4$ cup red onion, chopped

salt and pepper to taste

2 cups Ranch Dressing *(recipe below)*

1. Place the potatoes in a vegetable steamer or a basket set over boiling water. Do not let the potatoes touch the water. Cover and steam for 10 to 12 minutes, or until tender when poked with a sharp knife. When they are cool enough to handle, cut the potatoes into quarters.

2. Combine the potatoes, celery, and onion in a large bowl, and season with salt and pepper. Toss with enough dressing to moisten potatoes, and serve.

Serves 4 to 6.

RANCH DRESSING

At The Red Lion Inn this Ranch Dressing is used for several dishes — over a tossed salad, in place of mayonnaise in chicken sandwiches, and also in bacon, lettuce, and tomato sandwiches.

2 $^1/_2$ cups mayonnaise

$^1/_2$ cup sour cream

$^1/_2$ cup buttermilk

1 $^1/_2$ tablespoons garlic powder

2 $^1/_2$ tablespoons freeze-dried chives

dash salt

dash white pepper

1 drop Tabasco sauce

1. Combine all the ingredients in a bowl or jar and mix well. Refrigerate, covered, for at least 1 hour to allow the flavors to meld.

Yields 3 $^1/_2$ cups.

¹/₂ cup dried chickpeas

¹/₂ cup dried red kidney beans

¹/₂ cup dried black beans

¹/₂ cup dried white kidney beans

¹/₄ cup Spanish onions, diced

¹/₂ cup celery, diced

¹/₂ cup canned pimiento, diced

¹/₂ cup Red Lion Inn Robust Italian Dressing (*recipe follows*)

salt and pepper to taste

1 tablespoon fresh parsley, chopped

RED LION INN FOUR BEAN SALAD

This salad and dressing should be started the day before you plan to serve it, to allow time for the beans to soak and the dressing flavors to meld.

1. Wash and pick over the dried beans and discard any foreign material. In separate bowls, soak the chickpeas and each type of the beans overnight (a minimum of 4 hours) in water to cover by 2". (Or bring each to a boil in saucepans, and simmer for 2 minutes. Remove from heat and set aside to soak for 1 ¹/₂ to 2 hours.)

2. Combine the beans, along with the soaking water, in a large pot, leaving the chickpeas separate. Place the beans and the chickpeas on the stove and bring them to a boil. Reduce the heat and simmer for 1 hour, or until tender. Do not overcook. Watch closely, as the chickpeas will be done before the beans. Remove from heat, drain, and allow to cool.

3. Combine the beans and the chickpeas in a large bowl. Add the onions, celery, and pimiento. Stir in the dressing, tossing until the ingredients are well covered. Season to taste with salt and pepper, and sprinkle with the parsley. Allow the salad to sit covered and refrigerated for at least 4 hours before serving.

Serves 10 to 12.

APPLE HILL DESIGN

The Red Lion Inn's gift shop is called The Pink Kitty.

RED LION INN
ROBUST ITALIAN DRESSING

This classic salad dressing is a versatile one. It is excellent on a variety of salads, and can also be used as a marinade for steaks, chicken, and lamb kabobs.

1. Place the garlic, onion, parsley, and bell pepper in bowl, and add all spices and seasonings. Mix well.

2. Stir in the vinegar, and allow the dressing to stand for 10 minutes.

3. Whisk in the oil. Adjust the seasonings to taste, cover and refrigerate, and allow the dressing to stand at least 24 hours to meld the flavors.

Yields 4 cups.

3 cloves garlic, minced

4 tablespoons red onion, minced

2 tablespoons parsley, minced

3 tablespoons red bell pepper, minced

2 tablespoons dried basil

1 $^1/_2$ tablespoons garlic powder

1 tablespoon dried oregano

2 teaspoon crushed black pepper

$^1/_8$ teaspoon cayenne pepper

1 teaspoon salt

$^1/_4$ teaspoon dry mustard

1 cup red wine vinegar

3 cups olive oil

4 pounds vine-ripened tomatoes

2 cucumbers

2 medium Bermuda onions, thinly
   sliced

pinch of salt

fresh pepper to taste

4 tablespoons balsamic vinegar

1 cup extra virgin olive oil

2 tablespoons Parmesan cheese,
   grated

Fresh chopped parsley or basil
   (optional)

Chef's Fantastic Tomato, Cucumber, and Onion Salad

This recipe is marvelous when made in the heat of the Berkshire summer, when the tomatoes from the vine of a local garden have been sun-ripened and the cucumbers are crunchy fresh. It's terrific served with a crusty French bread and cheese.

1. Rinse and core the tomatoes. Cut them into quarters, saving all juice.

2. Slice the cucumbers in half lengthwise, and remove all seeds. Cut them into $1/2$" chunks.

3. Combine all the vegetables in a bowl, and sprinkle with the salt and pepper. Add the vinegar, toss, and let stand for 10 minutes. Add the olive oil. Toss well and drain off the excess dressing.

4. Sprinkle the vegetables with the Parmesan cheese (and parsley or basil, if desired) and serve on a cold plate.

Serves 4.

GRILLED SALMON AND ORANGE SALAD ON A BED OF SPINACH

4 salmon fillets, about $^1/_4$ pound each

$^1/_2$ cup teriyaki sauce

5 cups well-rinsed spinach leaves

4 navel orange

24 very thin slices red onion

2 tablespoons orange juice

8 scallions, tops removed, cut diagonally

1. Brush the salmon fillets with the teriyaki sauce and marinate them, covered, for 1 hour.

2. Place the spinach on a chilled plate.

3. Peel and section the oranges. Arrange orange sections and the onion slices around the greens. Refrigerate the plates while preparing the salmon.

4. Remove the salmon from the marinade, reserving the marinade for the dressing. Grill the salmon over a charcoal grill (or place under the broiler of an oven) until flaky — cook for 5 minutes on one side, brush with the reserved marinade, and grill for 4 minutes on the other side. (If the salmon fillets are more than $^3/_4$" thick, they may need more cooking time.) Place on a wire rack to cool slightly.

5. Prepare a dressing by combining 3 tablespoons of the reserved marinade with 2 tablespoons orange juice and whisk together well.

5. Place the hot, cooked salmon on the chilled greens, and sprinkle with the scallions. Drizzle the dressing over the salad and serve immediately.

Serves 4.

"Ate well but not wisely"

Frank Crowninshield, entry in the Red Lion Inn's guest book, October 11, 1941

1 cup apples (McIntosh are best),
   cored and sectioned

1 cup cranberries

1 cup sugar

1 package lemon gelatin dessert
   mix

1 cup hot water

1 cup pineapple juice

1/2 cup Tokay grapes, halved and
   seeded

1/4 cup walnuts, chopped

1 cup crushed canned pineapple,
   drained

Mayonnaise Dressing *(recipe below)*

CRANBERRY APPLE GELATIN SALAD

1. Grind the apples and cranberries in a food grinder or process in a food processor. Add the sugar and let stand 10 minutes.

2. Combine the lemon gelatin in 1 cup hot water in a large bowl, and stir until the gelatin has completely dissolved. Add the pineapple juice. Chill in the refrigerator until the gelatin has reached the soft set stage, from 1/2 hour to 1 hour.

3. Add the ground apples and cranberries, grapes, walnuts, and crushed pineapple to the gelatin, mixing well. Pour into decorative individual molds (or one large mold) and return the salad to the refrigerator to fully set.

4. Place each serving on a lettuce leaf, and drizzle the dressing over the top. Serve immediately.

Serves 8 to 10.

2 tablespoons mayonnaise

2 tablespoons heavy cream,
   whipped

1/2 teaspoon honey

pinch white pepper

MAYONNAISE DRESSING

1. Gently combine all ingredients together, and use immediately.

Yields 1/4 cup.

PASTA WITH BACON, BROCCOLI, AND MOZZARELLA

1. Cook the macaroni in boiling, salted water for 8 to 10 minutes, until tender. Drain thoroughly, and set aside to cool.

2. Blanch broccoli flowerets by dropping them into boiling water for 2 minutes. Drain, and cool in ice water, and drain again very thoroughly.

3. Combine the bacon, mozzarella, carrots, and onion in a salad bowl, and toss to mix well. Add the pasta and toss again. Then add the broccoli, and season with the garlic powder, salt, pepper, and onion powder.

4. Add the coleslaw dressing $^1/_2$ cup at a time, until the salad is lightly dressed and bound together. (If you will be serving it right away, 1 $^1/_2$ cups of dressing will be sufficient, but if you plan to hold it for a time, 2 cups may be needed.)

Serves 6 to 8.

3 cups dry elbow macaroni

1 head broccoli, cut into flowerets

$^1/_2$ pound bacon, cooked crisp

$^1/_2$ pound mozzarella, shredded

1 cup carrots, shredded

$^1/_2$ cup red onion, finely chopped

1 tablespoon garlic powder

salt and pepper to taste

1 teaspoon onion powder

1 $^1/_2$ to 2 cups Coleslaw Dressing *(see page 58)*

2 cups cabbage, finely grated

1 cup carrots, peeled and finely grated

$1/2$ cup Coleslaw Dressing *(recipe below)*

COLESLAW

A coleslaw of shredded cabbage and shredded carrots is a popular Red Lion Inn accompaniment to luncheon and dinner dishes, especially fish.

1. Combine the cabbage and carrots in a bowl.

2. Toss the vegetables with the coleslaw dressing and serve.

Serves 6.

2 cups mayonnaise

6 tablespoons maple syrup

4 tablespoons white vinegar

2 teaspoons paprika

4 tablespoons light cream

COLESLAW DRESSING

1. Combine all ingredients in a small bowl, and mix well. Cover the dressing and refrigerate. The dressing will keep under refrigeration 2 to 3 days.

Yields 2 $1/2$ cups.

BOWTIES WITH HAM, PEAS, AND PARMESAN DRESSING

1 pound dry bowtie pasta

2 tablespoons carrots, shredded

$^1/_4$ cup cooked ham, diced

$^1/_4$ cup cheddar cheese, diced

2 tablespoons frozen peas, thawed

1 cup Parmesan Dressing *(recipe below)*

This popular Red Lion Inn salad is best when served as soon as it is made. It will absorb the dressing if it is allowed to sit too long. (If that happens, just add more dressing before serving.)

1. Cook the pasta in boiling salted water for 8 to 10 minutes, or until tender. Drain well, and cool thoroughly.

2. Toss all the ingredients together until well mixed, and serve.

Serves 4 to 6.

PARMESAN DRESSING

$^1/_4$ cup Parmesan cheese, grated

$^1/_2$ cup heavy cream

1 cup mayonnaise

2 tablespoons garlic powder

salt and pepper to taste

1. Combine the grated Parmesan cheese and the cream in a small bowl, and allow it to stand for 10 minutes until the cheese has softened. Then stir in the mayonnaise and garlic powder, and season with salt and pepper. Mix well.

Yields 1 $^3/_4$ cups.

1 hard-boiled egg (optional)

2 sweet pickles

1 tablespoon onion, chopped

2 teaspoons red bell pepper, chopped

$^1/_2$ small green bell pepper, cored, seeded, and quartered

$^1/_2$ clove garlic, peeled

1 cup mayonnaise

$^1/_4$ cup chili sauce

$^1/_4$ teaspoon Worcestershire sauce

salt and pepper to taste

$^1/_4$ teaspoon Tabasco sauce

RED LION INN RUSSIAN DRESSING

Two salad dressings in particular generate many recipe requests at The Red Lion Inn. So even for those who haven't yet asked, here they are.

1. Grind the egg, pickles, onion, red pepper, green pepper, and garlic together in a food processor. Add the remaining ingredients and mix well. This dressing keeps under refrigeration for 1 week.

Yields 2 cups.

$^1/_2$ cup blue cheese, crumbled

$^1/_2$ cup sour cream

1 cup mayonnaise

$^1/_4$ cup buttermilk

1 tablespoon water

2 teaspoons white distilled vinegar

$^1/_8$ teaspoon Tabasco sauce

salt and pepper to taste

RED LION INN BLUE CHEESE DRESSING

1. Place $^1/_4$ cup of the crumbled blue cheese in a bowl. Add the other ingredients and mix well. Add the remaining blue cheese, and stir gently. This dressing keeps under refrigeration up to 10 days.

Yields 2 cups.

RED LION INN
LOW CALORIE DRESSING

1. Combine all ingredients in a jar or other covered container. Cover tightly and shake well to fully mix together. This dressing will keep in the refrigerator for up to 3 months.

Yields 5 cups.

4 cups cold water

1 tablespoon lemon juice

1 teaspoon Dijon-style mustard

$^3/_4$ teaspoon dried basil

$^3/_4$ teaspoon garlic powder

$^3/_4$ teaspoon dried oregano

pinch cayenne pepper

$^3/_4$ teaspoon dried tarragon

$^3/_4$ cup vinegar

$^1/_4$ cup apple juice

BREADS AND MUFFINS

In early New England, young girls learned to make bread just as their brothers learned to tend the plow. Bread was an essential part of a colonial meal. Having learned from her failure to make corn flour act just like wheat and rye flours, the New England housewife created distinctive breads of her own. Cornbread and brown bread, which must have wheat or rye flour added to the corn, bore little resemblance to the light, airy white breads of the old country, but were nevertheless suitable accompaniments to colonial dinners.

According to *The American Heritage Cookbook*, "Until the end of the eighteenth century, lightness in baked goods could be achieved only by laboriously beating air into dough along with eggs, or by adding yeast or spirits. In the 1790's, pearlash — a refined form of potash that produces carbon dioxide in baking dough — was discovered in America. Pearlash transformed baking methods: 8,000 tons of it was exported to Europe in 1792.

"It was not until the 1850's that baking powder (which worked in the same way as pearlash, except that it was new and improved) was commercially produced. In 1857, Professor E.N. Horsford of Harvard developed a formula for phosphate baking powder which moved Practical Housekeeping to declare, "Horsford's Bread Preparation saves time, simplifies the whole process of bread-making, saves labor, and reduces the chances of failure to the minimum.... It is certain that for rolls, biscuits, griddle-cakes, and the whole list of 'Breakfast and Tea Cakes,' the 'Bread Preparation' is superior to yeast or soda."

Quick breads, made with baking powder instead of yeast, were another way of using the abundance of New England harvests to advantage, and The Red Lion Inn has developed its own delightful versions, many of them shared here.

"To make good bread or to understand the process of making it is the duty of every woman; indeed an art that should never be neglected in the education of a lady. The lady derives her title from 'dividing or distributing bread'; the more perfect the bread the more perfect the lady."

Mrs. Sara Hale, Receipts for the Millions, 1857

PINEAPPLE BREAD

When New England sailing captains left the tropics of Polynesia to begin their return voyage, they often brought cases of pineapple with them. On their arrival home, the plump, juicy pineapples would be placed on the gatepost, signaling the safe return of the captain, and inviting friends in to celebrate with the family. This sign of "Open House" has been the symbol of hospitality ever since.

$^{1}/_{2}$ cup butter, softened

1 cup sugar

2 eggs

2 cups flour

1 teaspoon baking powder

pinch salt

1 cup canned crushed pineapple, drained

$^{1}/_{2}$ cup walnuts, chopped

1. Preheat the oven to 350°. Grease and flour two loaf pans.

2. Cream the butter and sugar together in a large mixing bowl. Beat the eggs in one at a time, and blend well after each addition.

3. Sift the flour, baking powder, and salt together. Add the flour mixture alternately with the crushed pineapple to the egg mixture. Stir in the nuts.

4. Pour the batter into the prepared loaf pans, and bake at 350° for 45 minutes to 1 hour, or until a toothpick inserted in the middle comes out clean.

Yields 2 small loaves.

4 eggs

2 ¹/₃ cups sugar

1 cup vegetable oil

2 cups canned pumpkin

3 cups flour

²/₃ teaspoon salt

1 ³/₄ teaspoons baking soda

2 ³/₄ teaspoons ground cinnamon

²/₃ teaspoon ground nutmeg

²/₃ teaspoon ground cloves

¹/₃ teaspoon ground allspice

1 cup chopped walnuts

¹/₃ cup golden raisins

¹/₄ cups sugar, for topping

1 teaspoon ground cinnamon, for topping

PUMPKIN BREAD OR MUFFINS

Pumpkin was one of the earliest vegetables the Pilgrims learned to grow. This form of squash was a plentiful Indian crop that apparently did not generate love at first sight. An early saying went: "We have pumpkins at morning, and pumpkins at noon; if it were not for pumpkins we should be undoon." Nevertheless, this recipe, served often at The Red Lion Inn, is a delicious use for that ageless crop. It works equally well as a loaf or as muffins.

1. Preheat the oven to 375°. Grease two loaf pans or twenty-four muffin cups.

2. Combine the eggs, sugar, oil, and pumpkin in a large bowl, and stir until smooth.

3. Sift the dry ingredients and spices together. Add to the egg mixture along with the walnuts and raisins, and mix thoroughly. Fill the loaf pans or muffin cups with the batter.

4. Mix the sugar and cinnamon together in a small bowl, and sprinkle over the bread or muffin batter.

5. Bake the bread at 375° for 1 hour and 10 minutes, or the muffins for 35 to 40 minutes. When the bread is done, a toothpick inserted in the center will come out clean.

Yields 2 loaves or 24 muffins.

CHEESE BREAD OR CLOVER LEAF CHEESE ROLLS

1/4 cup butter

1 cup diced onions

1 1/2 cups milk

2 tablespoons yeast

1 tablespoon salt

1/2 cup sugar

1/2 cup warm water

2 eggs

6 cups flour

2 cups extra sharp cheddar cheese, grated

2 tablespoons butter, melted

1. Preheat the oven to 350°. Grease two loaf pans or twenty-four muffin cups.

2. Melt the butter in a saucepan, and add the onions. Sauté over medium heat until soft, about 5 minutes. Stir in the milk, and let the mixture cool.

3. In a large bowl, combine the yeast, salt, sugar, and warm water (it should register about 105° on a candy thermometer). Stir well, and then set aside for about 10 minutes, or until the yeast has formed foamy bubbles on top.

4. Stir the onion mixture and the eggs into the yeast. Add the flour and cheese and mix thoroughly. Place the dough on a floured board and knead until it is no longer sticky, and has some elasticity, from 5 to 10 minutes. Place the dough in a greased stainless steel bowl. Cover the bowl with plastic wrap and set it in a warm, draft-free place. Let it rise until doubled in size, about 1 1/2 hours.

5. Punch the dough down. Place on a lightly floured board, and knead it briefly to release the air bubbles. Divide the dough in half, and shape each half into a loaf. Place them in the prepared loaf pans, cover with plastic wrap, and allow to rise again, until the bread fills the loaf pans, about 45 minutes. (For rolls, shape the dough into small balls so that three will fit into the bottom of each muffin cup. Cover and allow to rise until double in size.)

6. Brush the tops of the loaves with some of the melted butter, and bake in a 350° oven for 40 to 45 minutes, or until golden brown, and hollow-sounding if tapped. (For rolls, bake for 10 to 12 minutes or until golden brown.) Remove the pans from the oven, and immediately brush the bread with melted butter again. Allow the bread to cool in the pans for 10 minutes before unmolding them. Then cool on wire racks.

Yields 2 loaves or 24 rolls.

$^3/_4$ cup margarine, softened

1 cup sugar

2 eggs

3 cups flour

1 tablespoon baking powder

1 teaspoons salt

1 $^1/_3$ cups milk

1 cup blueberries, fresh or frozen

BLUEBERRY MUFFINS

New Englanders have an enduring devotion to blueberry muffins, as this passage illustrates: "In 1894, recalling a breakfast in Boston he had had some years earlier with Oliver Wendell Holmes's publisher, James T. Fields, William Dean Howells wrote, 'I remember his burlesque pretence that morning of an inextinguishable grief when I owned that I had never eaten blueberry cake [muffins] before, and how he kept returning to the pathos of the fact that there should be a region of the earth where blueberry cake was unknown.'" (*The American Heritage Cookbook*)

1. Preheat the oven to 375°. Grease twelve muffin cups.

2. In a large bowl, beat the margarine with $^3/_4$ cup of the sugar, until well blended. Add the eggs one at a time, creaming thoroughly after each addition, until light and fluffy.

3. In another bowl, combine 2 $^2/_3$ cups of the flour with the remaining dry ingredients. Add to the egg mixture and then add the milk. Mix just until moist. Do not overmix.

4. Place the remaining $^1/_3$ cup flour in a plastic bag. Add the berries to the bag and shake until the berries are lightly coated with flour. Add the berries to the batter. The batter will be very stiff if the berries are frozen. Drop the batter into the prepared muffin pans, filling them about two-thirds of the way. Sprinkle the remaining $^1/_4$ cup of sugar over the muffins.

5. Bake at 375° for 20 to 30 minutes, or until a toothpick inserted in the center comes out clean.

Yields 12 muffins.

RED LION INN LEMON BREAD

$^{3}/_{4}$ cup margarine

2 cups sugar

3 eggs

1 egg yolk

3 $^{1}/_{3}$ cups flour

1 tablespoon + $^{1}/_{2}$ teaspoon baking powder

1 $^{1}/_{2}$ teaspoons salt

2 cups Lemon Pudding (*recipe below*; or make from packaged mix, or purchase canned)

3 tablespoons milk

The Red Lion Inn's Lemon Bread is justifiably renowned. At lunch and dinner it's wrapped in a napkin and served in a basket along with the yeast rolls, offering a sweet alternative to traditional dinner rolls.

1. Preheat the oven to 350°. Grease two loaf pans.

2. In a large bowl, cream the margarine and sugar together thoroughly. Add the eggs, one at a time, mixing well after each.

3. Sift the dry ingredients together and add them to the eggs. Add the Lemon Pudding and milk, and mix until very well blended.

4. Pour the batter into the prepared loaf pans. Bake at 350° for 40 to 50 minutes, or until a toothpick inserted in the center comes out clean.

Yields 2 loaves.

LEMON PUDDING

3 tablespoons cornstarch

1 cup sugar

dash salt

1 $^{1}/_{2}$ cups warm water

$^{1}/_{2}$ cup lemon juice

4 egg yolks, beaten

1 tablespoon butter

1. In a heavy saucepan, mix the cornstarch, sugar, and salt, and stir together. Add the warm water and lemon juice. Cook over medium heat, stirring constantly, until the mixture comes to a boil.

2. Stir a small amount of the lemon mixture into the egg yolks, and then add the yolks to the pan. Cook but *do not boil* until thick, 6 to 8 minutes, stirring vigorously to retain the smooth consistency. Remove the pan from the heat.

3. Stir the butter into the lemon mixture until melted. Cover and allow to cool. The pudding will thicken more as it cools.

Yields 2 $^{1}/_{2}$ cups.

4 cups flour

2 cups sugar

1 teaspoon baking soda

1 tablespoon baking powder

2 teaspoons salt

$^1/_2$ cup margarine

1 $^1/_2$ cups orange juice

2 tablespoons orange peel, grated

2 eggs, beaten

1 cup walnuts, chopped

4 cups cranberries, chopped

CRANBERRY ORANGE NUT BREAD

The Pilgrims found cranberries growing wild when they arrived in their new country, and they immediately began adapting them to various uses. Massachusetts is still the cranberry capital and this recipe is a delightful way to use this typically New England crop.

1. Preheat the oven to 375°. Grease two loaf pans.

2. Sift all the dry ingredients together in a large bowl. Cut in the margarine, using a pastry blender, until it is about the size of a small pea.

3. Mix the orange juice, orange peel, and eggs together in another bowl, and then combine the mixture with the flour, stirring well. Fold in the nuts and cranberries.

4. Pour the batter into the prepared loaf pans, and bake at 375° for 1 hour or until a toothpick inserted in the center comes out clean. Let the loaves cool in the pans, then wrap them in plastic wrap and let them rest overnight (this improves the flavor and makes slicing easier).

Yields 2 loaves.

ORANGE BREAD

1. Preheat oven to 350°. Grease one loaf pan.

2. Peel the orange and remove the seeds. Remove the pits from the dates. Grind the orange pulp, dates, and nuts together in a food processor or a food grinder. Set the mixture aside.

3. Whip the butter, warm water, and egg together in a large bowl. Sift together the flour, baking powder, baking soda, salt, and sugar, and add the dry ingredients to the liquids. Blend all together well. Add the date mixture, and combine thoroughly.

4. Pour the batter into the greased loaf pan, and bake at 350° for 40 to 50 minutes, or until a toothpick inserted in the center comes out clean.

Yields 1 loaf.

1 medium orange

²/₃ cup dates

¹/₂ cup walnuts

2 tablespoons butter

¹/₂ cup warm water

1 egg

2 cups flour

1 ¹/₂ teaspoons baking powder

¹/₃ teaspoon baking soda

¹/₄ teaspoon salt

³/₄ cup sugar

Collection of Teapots, Red Lion Inn,   Stockbridge, Mass.

The famous Red Lion Inn collection of teapots, in a vintage postcard.

1 cup lukewarm water

1 tablespoon dry yeast

1 tablespoon sugar

1 $1/4$ teaspoons salt

2 tablespoons vegetable oil

3 cups flour

2 tablespoons cornmeal

1 cup hot water

1 $1/2$ teaspoons cornstarch

"The Red Lion, at Stockbridge, made us welcome, and after Mr. Mears and I had gone to our rooms and bathed and dressed, we met in the lobby and went in to dinner. He requested milk toast 'and a can of sardines, unopened, but be sure to bring me the key.' Evidently, the Red Lion staff is accustomed to visitors of great peculiarity or else had dealt with Mr. Mears before, because no one so much as lifted an eyebrow. Mr. Mears dumped the sardines onto the milk toast, stirred the mixture into a sort of paste, and ate it mechanically. I had a steak dinner, which I enjoyed very much, having developed a technique for the occasion. My technique consisted simply of not looking at Mr. Mears any more than I could help...."

James Reid Parker, The New Yorker, September 4, 1948

FRENCH BREAD OR KNOTTED FRENCH ROLLS

1. Grease a sheet pan.

2. Whisk the lukewarm water, yeast, sugar, salt, and oil together in a large bowl. Add 1 $1/2$ cups of the flour, and beat until blended. Gather the dough into ball.

3. Knead the dough on a floured bread board or countertop, adding the remaining 1 $1/2$ cups flour until all is blended in. This will probably take about 10 minutes. The dough should be pliable and elastic.

4. Place the dough in a greased bowl, turning once to coat the dough, and cover it. Let the dough rise in a warm place, until it has doubled in size (about 1 hour).

5. Punch the dough down, return it to the bowl, cover it, and let it rise until doubled again (about 30 minutes).

6. Divide the dough in half, and let it rest for 10 minutes. Press each portion out flat and roll it up jelly-roll style to form a long loaf. Sprinkle the greased sheet pan with the cornmeal, and place the loaves on the cornmeal. Allow them to rise again, covered with a light towel, in a warm place, until double (about 20 to 30 minutes).

   (For rolls: after the dough has been divided in half and has rested, divide each half into twelve sections. Roll each section into a 5" rope and tie each rope into a knot. Allow to rise. Bake for 10 to 12 minutes or until golden brown, brushing with the cornstarch mixture halfway through cooking.)

7. Preheat the oven to 450°. Combine the hot water with the cornstarch in a saucepan, and heat it for 1 to 2 minutes. Allow the mixture to cool to room temperature.

8. Score diagonal cuts on the tops of the loaves with a sharp knife, and brush them with some of the cornstarch mixture. Place the sheet pan of bread in the oven, and place a pan of water on the rack below it. Bake at 450° for 10 minutes. Brush the loaves with the cornstarch mixture again, and bake another 25 minutes. When it's done, the bread will sound hollow when tapped.

Yields 2 loaves or 24 rolls.

MIKE'S BRAN MUFFINS

Michael Terranova has been a chef at The Red Lion Inn for ten years. His inventive recipes, including these popular bran muffins, are a distinctive addition to the Red Lion Inn's repertoire. The batter for these muffins should be prepared the night before you're going to bake them.

1. Cream the margarine and sugar together thoroughly in a large bowl. Add the eggs, and cream well again.

2. Sift the flour. Add the flour to the egg mixture, alternating with the buttermilk, mixing well after each addition.

3. Dissolve the baking soda in hot water. Add it to the batter, and mix well. Then add bran flakes and all-bran. The batter will be rather thin. Allow it to sit covered in the refrigerator overnight.

4. Preheat the oven to 350°. Grease eighteen muffin cups.

5. Just before baking, add the carrots and raisins to the batter. Pour the batter into the prepared muffin cups, and bake at 350° for 30 to 40 minutes, or until a toothpick inserted in the center comes out clean. Allow the muffins to cool for 10 minutes before removing them from the cups.

Yields 18 muffins.

½ cup margarine

1 cup sugar

2 eggs, beaten

2 ¾ cups flour

2 cups buttermilk

2 ½ teaspoons baking soda

1 cup hot water

1 cup bran flakes

2 cups all-bran

1 ¼ cups carrots, finely grated

½ cup raisins

1 cup dried apricot halves

1 cup orange juice

¹/₄ cup butter or margarine

³/₄ cup sugar

1 egg

¹/₂ cup milk

1 cup whole bran cereal

2 teaspoons grated orange peel

¹/₄ cup slivered blanched almonds

2 cups sifted flour

1 tablespoon baking powder

¹/₂ teaspoon baking soda

¹/₂ teaspoon salt

APRICOT NUT BREAD

1. Preheat the oven to 325°. Grease one loaf pan.

2. Dice the apricots into ¹/₄" pieces. Combine the apricots and the orange juice in a small saucepan, and cook over moderately low heat until the mixture comes to a boil. Continue cooking 5 minutes. Then remove the pan from the heat, and allow the mixture to cool.

3. In a large bowl, cream together the butter and sugar. Add the egg and milk, and mix until well blended. Stir in the bran, orange peel, apricot mixture, and nuts, mixing well.

4. Sift the flour, baking powder, baking soda, and salt together. Add the dry ingredients to the apricot mixture, and stir until thoroughly moistened.

5. Pour the batter into the prepared pan, and bake at 325° for 55 to 60 minutes, or until a toothpick inserted in the center comes out clean.

Yields 1 loaf.

APPLE CIDER BREAD OR MUFFINS

The flavor of this recipe will improve if the baked bread is allowed to rest for 24 hours after it is baked.

1. Preheat the oven to 375°. Grease and flour two loaf pans or eighteen muffin cups.

2. Cream the butter and 1 ¼ cup of the sugar together in a large bowl. Add eggs and cream thoroughly.

3. Sift the dry ingredients together. Add them to the egg mixture, alternating with the apple cider. Stir in the chopped apples.

4. Divide the batter between the prepared loaf pans. Combine the remaining ¼ cup sugar with the cinnamon in a small bowl, and sprinkle it over the batter.

5. Bake at 375° for 50 to 70 minutes for bread, or for 30 to 40 minutes for muffins, or until a toothpick inserted in the center comes out clean.

Yields 2 loaves or 18 muffins.

1 cup butter

1 ½ cups sugar

3 eggs

4 cups flour

1 ½ tablespoons baking powder

1 ½ teaspoons salt

1 ½ teaspoons cinnamon

2 cups apple cider

2 cups apples, peeled, cored, and chopped

1 teaspoon cinnamon

³/₄ cup butter

1 ³/₄ cups sugar

3 whole eggs

1 egg yolk

5 large ripe bananas, peeled and mashed

3 ¹/₂ cups flour

1 ¹/₂ teaspoons salt

1 tablespoon + 1 teaspoon baking powder

¹/₂ cup walnuts, chopped

BANANA NUT BREAD OR MUFFINS

Bananas were introduced to America by a New England sea captain, Lorenzo Baker of Wellfleet, Massachusetts. He first brought back only one bunch of green bananas from Jamaica, but they were so well received that he eventually gave up seafaring and went into the banana business full time.

1. Preheat the oven to 350°. Butter two loaf pans or eighteen muffin cups.

2. Cream the butter and sugar together in a large bowl. Beat in the eggs, one at a time, creaming well after each addition.

3. Mix the mashed bananas into the egg mixture. At this point the batter will appear to "break" and become soupy.

4. Sift all the dry ingredients together and add them to the egg mixture. Mix gently to combine. Add the walnuts.

5. Pour the batter into the prepared pans. Bake the bread at 350° for 50 to 60 minutes, or the muffins for 25 to 30 minutes, or until a toothpick inserted in the center comes out clean.

Yields 2 loaves or 18 muffins.

YEAST ROLLS

Although this recipe may easily be divided in half, Chef Mongeon believes it is best made in a larger quantity to retain the necessary sweetness. These rolls will freeze beautifully, available for dinner on a moment's notice.

4 cups milk

1 ¹/₂ ounces yeast

6 tablespoons sugar

¹/₂ teaspoon salt

6 cups flour

1 egg white

¹/₄ cup milk

1. Lightly grease a baking sheet.

2. Place the milk in a saucepan and heat over low heat until it reads 105° on a candy thermometer. Pour the hot milk into a large mixing bowl and sprinkle it with the yeast, and stirring well. Allow it to sit about 10 minutes to dissolve the yeast. Small bubbles and foam should form quickly.

3. Add the sugar and salt, then add 1 cup of the flour at a time, until a sticky dough is created. When it is too difficult to mix, add the remaining flour by kneading on a floured bread board.

4. Place the dough in a large, greased, stainless steel bowl, turning the dough once to grease all sides. Cover the bowl with plastic wrap and let the dough rise in a warm, draft-free place until it has doubled in size, about 1 hour.

5. Preheat the oven to 400°. Punch the dough down, and knead it again for a few minutes, just to release the air pockets. Cut or pull off small portions of dough, and roll each into a small ball (or you can roll each portion into a short rope and tie in a knot). Place the formed rolls on the prepared baking sheet. Cover with plastic wrap, and allow to rise in a warm, draft-free place until double in size, about 18 to 20 minutes.

6. Prepare an egg wash by whipping egg white and milk together in a small bowl. Brush the tops of the rolls with the egg wash, and bake them in a 400° oven for 10 to 12 minutes, or until golden brown.

7. If you are planning to freeze the rolls, either freeze the raw dough, or partially bake the rolls for about 8 minutes, and then freeze. Finish baking the rolls just before serving.

Yields 10 dozen rolls.

"Papa didn't like baker's bread and I determined to learn to make homemade bread for him. It took all summer. Mixing was heavy work and baking a hot, hard chore. But there came a day when I took from the oven a perfect loaf, beautifully brown and light as a feather. I wrapped it in a snowy napkin and presented it to my father."

New England Cookbook

CHALLAH

1 package dry yeast

$1/4$ cup lukewarm water

3 tablespoons vegetable oil

1 tablespoon sugar

1 teaspoon salt

$1/3$ cup water, at room temperature

3 egg yolks, beaten

2 $1/4$ to 2 $3/4$ cups flour

1 egg yolk, for egg wash

2 tablespoons water, for egg wash

1. Grease a baking sheet.

2. Dissolve the yeast in the lukewarm water in large bowl. Set it aside for 10 minutes. The yeast should be bubbly and foamy.

3. Whisk in the 2 tablespoons of the oil, sugar, salt, and $1/3$ cup additional water. Add the egg yolks. Using an electric mixer, beat the ingredients together, also adding 1 $1/4$ cups of the flour.

4. Stir in enough additional flour to make the dough firm enough to handle, about $3/4$ cup. Let the dough rest, covered, for 10 minutes. Then knead the dough on a floured board for 8 to 10 minutes, adding additional flour until the dough is smooth and shiny. Place it a greased bowl, turning the dough to grease all sides, cover the bowl with plastic wrap and place it in a warm, draft-free place, allowing it to rise until doubled in size, from 40 minutes to 1 hour.

5. Divide the dough into thirds, cover again, and let rest 10 minutes. Then, with your hands, roll the dough on a floured surface, forming three ropes of dough of equal length, approximately 18". Laying the ropes of dough on the prepared baking sheet, press all three together at the top and then braid them together.

6. Brush the braided loaf lightly with the remaining tablespoon of oil and let it rise, covered, for 30 to 40 minutes. (The bread will not double in size this time.)

7. Preheat the oven to 375°. Whisk the egg yolk and the water together in a small bowl to form an egg wash, and brush the loaf lightly with the mixture.

8. Bake at 375° for 25 minutes, or until it sounds hollow when tapped lightly.

Yields 1 loaf.

MEAT AND GAME

From the earliest times, New Englanders have depended on game for their dinner table. Wild turkeys, which roamed the New England countryside, and still can be seen in Berkshire fields, held a special place in American hearts — and still do.

Benjamin Franklin once wrote to his daughter, Sarah Bache, "I wish the Bald Eagle had not been chose as the Representation of our Country; he is a Bird of bad moral Character, like those among men who live by sharpening and robbing, he is generally poor and often very lousy.... The turkey is...a much more respectable bird, and withal a true original Native of America."

Turkeys will always be associated with Thanksgiving — from that first Pilgrim celebration to today. Edward Winslow described the first Thanksgiving in 1621: "Our harvest being gotten in, our governor sent four men on fowling, that so we might, after a special manner, rejoice together after we had gathered the fruit of our labors. They four in one day killed as much fowl as, with a little help beside, served the company almost a week. At which time, among other recreations, we exercised our arms, many of the Indians coming among us, and amongst the rest their greatest king, Massasoit, with some 90 men, whom for three days we...feasted. And they went out and killed five deer, which they brought to the plantation and bestowed on our Governor and upon the Captain and others."

This description may sound like a magnificent feast, but according to *American Cooking: New England*, "The first Thanksgiving is often depicted as a lavish feast, with outdoor tables laden with all sorts of delicacies, but it could not have been anything of the sort. Plymouth at that time was a tiny cluster of huts, built mostly of sod and thatch. The colonists had few possessions beyond the simplest tools and household equipment, and the stores they had brought from England were practically exhausted. Most likely they entertained their Indian friends with fish and game, including the deer that the guests contributed, and corn and beans cooked in the Indian manner."

In addition to turkey, game birds, venison, and fish, New Englanders devised another thrifty and easy dinner that enjoyed considerable popularity. Traditionally, a New England boiled dinner consists of boiled corned beef,

"Sir, respect your dinner; idolize it, enjoy it properly. You will be by many hours in the week, many weeks in the year, and many years in your life the happier if you do."

William Makepeace Thackeray, Memorials of Gormandizing

cabbage, and other vegetables, served with a side dish of beets. Leftovers can be used for corned beef hash for breakfast the next day. If the meat is ground with the leftover beets, it will turn the hash a bright red, which the Pilgrims called Red Flannel Hash. The Red Lion Inn continues to serve a traditional New England Boiled Dinner every St. Patrick's Day.

During the summer months, when the courtyard at The Red Lion Inn is open for dinner, Tuesday is Steak Night. That's the night when the outdoor grill is stoked and steaks are cooked to order, accompanied by a salad bar. As the sun goes down, and the tables are lit with white hurricane candles, it's a delightful place for a relaxing summer meal.

Sarah Knight apparently had a most unpleasant journey from Boston to New York in 1704. She wrote that she "paid six-pence for our dinner which was nothing but smell." In another entry in her diary about a meal of pork and cabbage, she described a "sauce of deep purple, which I thought was boiled in a dye kettle."

VEAL SCALLOPS WITH MUSHROOMS, HAM, AND CHEESE

1. Preheat the broiler.

2. Heat $^1/_4$ cup of the butter in a large skillet, sauté 2 tablespoons of the shallots over medium heat until soft, about 2 to 3 minutes. Stir in the mushrooms and sauté until moisture has evaporated, about 10 minutes. Then stir in $^2/_3$ cup of the cream, and season with the salt and pepper. Cook, stirring occasionally, until the cream is reduced by half, and the sauce has thickened considerably, about 10 minutes. Keep warm.

3. Sprinkle the veal with salt and pepper, and dust with flour.

4. Melt the remaining $^1/_4$ cup butter in another skillet, and sauté the cutlets over medium heat for 2 minutes on each side, or until cooked through. Transfer them to a flameproof gratin dish and keep warm.

5. Pour off any butter remaining in the skillet. Add the remaining 2 tablespoons shallots and the wine, scraping up the brown bits on the bottom of the pan. Reduce the mixture by one-third over high heat, about 4 minutes. Stir in the remaining 1 $^1/_3$ cups cream and cook until the mixture is reduced by one-half, and has thickened considerably, about 10 minutes. Season with salt and pepper to taste.

6. Top each cutlet with some of the creamed mushrooms, then some julienned ham, 2 slices of cheese, and the sauce. Broil for 2 minutes and serve immediately.

Serves 4.

$^1/_2$ cup butter

4 tablespoons shallots, minced

1 pound mushrooms, sliced

2 cups heavy cream

4 veal cutlets (6 ounces each), pounded $^3/_{16}$" thick

salt and pepper to taste

flour

$^2/_3$ cup dry white wine

4 thin slices cooked ham, julienned

8 thin slices Swiss cheese

³/₄ cup butter

¹/₂ cup flour

1 ¹/₂ pounds venison, cut into steaks or medallions about ¹/₄" to ¹/₂" thick

³/₄ cup fresh shiitake mushrooms

³/₄ cup fresh oyster mushrooms

2 teaspoons black peppercorns, cracked (see Step 3)

4 tablespoons shallots, minced

2 teaspoons thyme

¹/₄ cup red wine

¹/₄ cup Glace de Viande (*recipe follows*)

SIRLOIN OF VENISON WITH RED WINE SAUCE

This hearty, peppery dish is a favorite of Red Lion Inn guests, especially in the late fall.

1. Heat ¹/₂ cup of the butter in a sauté pan. Dredge the venison in the flour, and sauté it over medium heat, turning once, until cooked to your taste (rare is best, 6 to 8 minutes). Remove the meat from the pan and keep it warm.

2. Wipe the mushrooms clean and discard the stems. Slice the shiitake mushroom caps. Add all the mushroom caps to the sauté pan and cook until the liquid they create has evaporated, about 5 minutes.

3. Meanwhile, crack the peppercorns by placing them on a cutting board and pressing firmly with the bottom of a heavy skillet. Add the cracked pepper, shallots, thyme, and red wine to the pan with the mushrooms. Cook over high heat until reduced by half, about 3 minutes.

4. Add the Glace de Viande, and then swirl in the remaining ¹/₄ cup butter. Heat, but do not allow to boil or it will separate. Pour the sauce over the venison and serve immediately.

Serves 4.

GLACE DE VIANDE

2 cups beef stock (*see page 37*)

Glace de Viande is a syrupy, strong-flavored derivative of a basic stock. It can be made from beef, chicken, or veal stock. A little bit will add a rich flavor to any dish.

1. Place the beef stock in a saucepan over high heat and bring to a boil. Reduce to a simmer and continue to cook (skimming any fat from the surface) until it is reduced to a very thick, dark consistency, about 5 to 6 hours.

2. Use immediately, or allow it to cool (it will have a rubbery quality). Store in the refrigerator, tightly wrapped in plastic wrap, until ready to use. It will keep up to three months.

Yields $^1/_4$ cup.

12 asparagus spears

4 veal cutlets, pounded very thin

flour

salt and pepper

2 tablespoons butter

1 cup cooked lobster meat

Hollandaise Sauce (*recipe below*)

VEAL OSCAR

1. In a vegetable steamer, steam the asparagus spears just until cooked, but still crisp, about 5 minutes. Set them aside.

2. Dredge the veal in flour seasoned with salt and pepper.

3. Heat the butter in a skillet, and sauté the veal over medium-high heat for two minutes on each side. Transfer the meat to a serving platter or individual plates.

4. Place a portion of the lobster meat on top of each piece of veal, and top each serving with three asparagus spears. Spoon Hollandaise Sauce over the top and serve.

Serves 4.

4 egg yolks

4 ½ tablespoons fresh lemon juice

2 tablespoons cold water

1 cup clarified butter, melted (*see page 25*)

salt and cayenne pepper to taste

¼ teaspoon Worcestershire sauce

HOLLANDAISE SAUCE

1. Place egg yolks, lemon juice, and water in a stainless steel bowl over boiling water, or use a double boiler. Cook, whisking with a wire whisk, until the mixture has a light custard consistency, from 10 to 15 minutes. Remove from the heat and whip until the custard falls slightly, about 1 minute.

2. Slowly whisk in the melted butter, a little at a time. Season with salt, cayenne, and Worcestershire sauce. Use immediately, or will keep in the refrigerator for 2 to 3 days.

Yields 1 ½ cup.

Roast Long Island Duckling with Cranberry Glaze

1. Preheat the oven to 325°. Spray the rack of a roasting pan with spray cooking oil.

2. Remove the neck and giblets from the duck, and trim off any excess skin and fat. Rinse out the cavity and pat dry. Combine the apple, onion, lemon, orange, and bay leaves together in a bowl, and then place them in the duck cavity. Prick the top and sides of the duck with a fork (this allows the fat to drain while the duck is roasting). Season the skin with salt and pepper.

3. Place the duck in the prepared pan, and roast for 3 hours at 325°. Remove it from the oven and drain off all the fat, reserving it for the Duck Espagnole. Lower the heat to 250° and return the duck to the oven.

4. Mix the honey, soy sauce, and ginger together. Cook the duck for an additional 10 minutes, basting with this mixture twice. Serve with Cranberry Demi-Glace.

Serves 4.

1 Long Island Duckling (5 $^1/_2$ to 6 pounds)

$^1/_2$ apple, peeled, cored, and diced

1 small onion, peeled and diced

$^1/_8$ lemon, peeled, sectioned and diced

$^1/_4$ orange, peeled, sectioned and diced

2 bay leaves

salt and pepper

2 tablespoons honey

3 tablespoons soy sauce

pinch ground ginger

Cranberry Demi-Glace (*recipe follows*)

"Will Hawkins used to shoot quail and partridge during open season for The Red Lion Inn table...."

The Springfield Union, September 12, 1943

¼ cup sugar

1 tablespoon lemon juice

2 tablespoons orange juice

6 tablespoons cranberry juice

1 tablespoon currant jelly

¼ cup Cointreau

4 cups Duck Espagnole (*recipe follows*)

1 bag cranberries, 12 ounces

CRANBERRY DEMI-GLACE

1. Caramelize the sugar by cooking it in a saucepan over medium heat until it melts and turns a light brown color, 5 to 6 minutes. Be careful it doesn't burn! Remove the pan from the heat.

2. Add the remaining ingredients except the cranberries to the sugar, being careful it doesn't splatter. The caramel will harden, but stir the mixture together thoroughly and return it to the heat. As the ingredients warm, the caramel mixture will soften. Cook over medium heat until reduced by one-third, about 40 minutes, stirring occasionally.

3. Add the cranberries and boil until they pop, about 5 to 6 minutes.

Yields 2 ½ to 3 cups.

DUCK ESPAGNOLE

1. Heat the duck fat in a large soup pot, and add the onion, carrot, celery, garlic, shallots, and tomato. Sauté over low heat for about 30 minutes, or until the vegetables are light brown and tender.

2. Add the tomato paste, bay leaves, thyme, pepper, and rosemary, and cook 10 minutes more. Then add the stock and simmer for 2 hours.

3. Make a roux by melting the butter in a small saucepan. Add the flour, and stir to create a paste. Cook over medium heat for 2 to 3 minutes.

4. Add the roux to the stock and cook for 1 hour longer, until the sauce is thickened and reduced to 1 quart.

5. Skim off any fat, strain, and add salt to taste.

Yields 4 cups.

$1/4$ cup duck fat

$1/2$ onion, peeled and chopped

1 carrot, peeled and chopped

2 stalks celery, chopped

1 clove garlic, diced

2 shallots, peeled and chopped

1 tomato, chopped

2 tablespoons tomato paste

2 bay leaves

1 teaspoon dried thyme

1 teaspoon pepper

1 teaspoon dried rosemary

2 quarts duck or chicken stock (*see page 38*)

1 cup butter

1 cup flour

dash salt

4 veal cutlets, 6 to 8 ounces each

$^1/_2$ cup flour

$^1/_2$ cup butter

$^1/_2$ cup white wine

2 tablespoons lemon juice

$^1/_4$ cup capers

$^1/_2$ cup butter, cold

4 teaspoons parsley, chopped

VEAL PICATTA

1. Pound the cutlets until thin, and dredge them in flour.

2. Melt the butter in a sauté pan, over medium-high heat. Sauté the veal for 2 minutes on each side. Transfer the veal to a platter and keep warm.

3. Add the wine, lemon juice, and capers to the sauté pan, and boil until reduced to a syrup, about 5 minutes.

4. Remove the pan from the heat and add the cold butter. Melt it by gently shaking the pan so as not to let the sauce separate. Pour the sauce over the veal, sprinkle with the chopped parsley, and serve immediately.

Serves 4.

Roast Christmas Goose with Orange Gravy

A fat goose was the traditional English Michaelmas fare from the time of Elizabeth I, and later became a Christmas tradition as well. The Red Lion Inn's Christmas goose recreates that early beloved tradition.

1. Preheat the oven to 350°.

2. Clean the goose by removing the neck, liver, giblets, heart, and all fat from the cavity. Thoroughly rinse out the cavity and pat dry. Singe off any feathers.

3. Combine the onions, oranges, lemons, apples, and bay leaves together in a bowl, then place them in the goose cavity. Season with salt and pepper. (This stuffing is for flavor only. It will not be served.)

4. Truss the bird to hold the legs together. Prick the skin well around the legs and back (this will allow the fat to drain during cooking). Rub the skin well with salt and pepper. Place the goose on a rack in a roasting pan.

5. Roast the goose for approximately 12 minutes per pound at 350° (2 $^1/_2$ to 2 $^3/_4$ hours). Baste it with boiling water twice during the first hour to help render out the fat. Drain the fat as it accumulates in the pan, reserving it for the demi-glace. When a meat thermometer registers 180°, remove the pan from the oven, and transfer the goose to a heated platter. Cover the goose with foil and allow it to rest for at least 10 minutes. Drain the fat from the roasting pan, but reserve it. Add the white wine to the pan, scraping up the brown bits on the bottom. Add this liquid to the goose demi-glace for the gravy.

6. To serve, carve the goose into individual slices, and serve Apple Apricot Chestnut Dressing and Orange Gravy on the side.

Serves 8 to 10.

---

1 goose (12 to 14 pounds)

2 large onions, peeled and cut into large chunks

2 oranges, peeled and sectioned

2 lemons, peeled and sectioned

2 McIntosh apples, quartered (do not peel)

3 bay leaves

salt and pepper to taste

$^1/_2$ cup white wine

Goose Demi-Glace (*recipe follows*)

Orange Gravy (*recipe follows*)

Apple-Apricot Chestnut Dressing (*recipe follows*)

¹/₄ cup sugar

¹/₄ cup red wine vinegar

¹/₂ cup + 3 tablespoons orange juice

2 oranges

5 cups Goose Demi-Glace (*recipe below*)

1 lemon

2 tablespoons red currant jelly

¹/₄ cup Cointreau

1 cup goose fat (reserved drippings)

1 cup onions, chopped

¹/₂ cup celery, chopped

¹/₂ cup carrots, chopped

1 cup flour

8 cups goose or chicken stock (*see page 38*)

5 to 10 parsley stems

3 bay leaves

2 teaspoons tomato paste

¹/₂ cup white wine

salt and pepper to taste

ORANGE GRAVY

1. Caramelize the sugar by cooking it in a saucepan over medium heat until it melts and turns a light brown color, 5 to 6 minutes. Be careful it doesn't burn! Remove the pan from the heat. Add the vinegar and orange juice, being careful it doesn't splatter. The caramel will harden, but stir the mixture together thoroughly and return it to the heat; then the caramel mixture will soften. Simmer until it has reduced by half, about 15 minutes.

2. Peel the orange, removing only the zest (no white pith) and cut the peel into thin strips. Place strips in a saucepan, cover with water, and simmer for 2 minutes. Drain, and add the peel to the sauce.

3. Add the demi-glace to the sauce, and simmer for 10 minutes. Squeeze the juice from the oranges and the lemon, and add it to the sauce. Stir in the currant jelly and Cointreau. Simmer an additional 5 minutes, and season with salt and pepper.

Yields 5 to 5 ¹/₂ cups.

GOOSE DEMI-GLACE

1. Heat the fat in a stockpot, add the vegetables, and sauté over medium heat, until lightly browned and syrupy, about 15 minutes. Add the flour and cook for 10 minutes, until the flour turns a nice nutty color.

2. Add the stock, parsley stems, bay leaves, tomato paste, white wine, and salt and pepper, and bring to a boil. Simmer for 1 ¹/₂ hours, skimming the fat from the top as it rises, until reduced to 5 cups.

Yields 5 cups.

APPLE APRICOT CHESTNUT DRESSING

1. Preheat the oven to 350°. Butter a 3-quart casserole dish.

2. Melt the butter or drippings in a large saucepan. Sauté the onions and celery over medium heat until tender, about 5 minutes; then add the apples and sauté for 2 minutes. Remove the pan from the heat.

3. Add the bread cubes, apricots, chestnuts, parsley, salt, and paprika. Toss until the mixture is moist but not wet.

4. Place the dressing in the prepared casserole, and bake at 350° for 1 hour. If it seems too dry, moisten it with a little stock, while baking.

Yields 8 cups.

1 cup butter or goose fat

1 cup onions, diced

$^1/_2$ cup celery, diced

2 cups McIntosh apples, peeled, cored, and diced

6 cups bread, cubed (crusts removed)

1 $^1/_2$ cups apricots, diced

1 cup chestnuts, peeled, boiled, and chopped

$^1/_4$ cup parsley, chopped

2 teaspoons salt

1 teaspoon paprika

$^1/_4$ cup goose stock, or chicken stock (*see page 38*)

1 beef rib roast (19 to 20 pounds)

1 tablespoon salt

$1/2$ teaspoon black pepper

$1/2$ teaspoon white pepper

1 tablespoon dried thyme

1 tablespoon garlic powder

$1/2$ cup Worcestershire sauce

2 cups onion, diced

$1/2$ cup carrots, diced

$1/2$ cup celery, diced

6 to 8 parsley stems, chopped

1 tomato, peeled and diced

2 cups beef stock (*see page 37*)

ROAST PRIME RIB OF BEEF

1. Prepare a seasoning mix by combining the salt, peppers, thyme, and garlic powder in a small bowl.

2. Sprinkle the Worcestershire sauce and then the seasoning mix over the meat; rub it in with your hands. Let the roast stand in the refrigerator for at least 3 hours.

3. One hour before cooking time, remove the roast from the refrigerator and let it come to room temperature.

4. Preheat the oven to 350°. Place the roast on a rack in a roasting pan and add the vegetables to the pan surrounding the roast. Bake for 1 $1/2$ hour, or until a meat thermometer registers 120°.

5. Remove the roast from the pan, and allow it to rest in a warm place, covered with foil, for 30 minutes before carving.

6. Meanwhile, drain the grease from the roasting pan, leaving the vegetables in the pan. Add the beef stock to the pan, scraping with a spoon until all the drippings are loosened. Simmer over medium heat on top of the stove, for 10 minutes. Strain. Serve this "au jus" sauce as an accompaniment to the roast.

Serves 16.

CALVES LIVER
WITH BACON AND ONIONS

1. Season the flour with salt and pepper and dredge the liver in the flour, shaking off any excess.

2. Heat the oil or drippings in a sauté pan and add the liver. Sauté the liver over medium high heat for 5 minutes, then turn and sauté for 4 minutes on the other side. Transfer the liver to a heated platter and keep warm.

3 Reduce the heat to medium and add the onions to the pan; season with salt and pepper and cook until tender, about 5 minutes. Arrange the onions over the liver, top with the bacon strips, and serve.

Serves 4.

$^1/_2$ cup flour

salt and pepper to taste

$^3/_4$ cup vegetable oil or bacon drippings

1 $^1/_2$ to 2 pounds calves liver (8 pieces)

2 small onions, thinly sliced

8 strips bacon, cooked

1 medium turkey, and neck,
  giblets, gizzard, heart, and liver
  (about 10 pounds)

Bread Stuffing (*recipe follows*)

¹/₄ **cup butter or margarine**

1 teaspoon salt

¹/₄ **teaspoon pepper**

1 teaspoon poultry seasoning

1 teaspoon sage

Pan Gravy (*recipe follows*)

Mrs. Stephen Johnson Field, whose husband was from Stockbridge and was appointed a Supreme Court Justice by President Lincoln, wrote a book in 1890 entitled Statesmen's Dishes and How to Cook Them. *Her secret ingredients for a Christmas turkey: "The turkey should be cooped up and fed some time before Christmas. Three days before it is slaughtered, it should have an English walnut forced down its throat three times a day, and a glass of sherry once a day. The meat will be deliciously tender, and have a fine nutty flavor."*

ROAST TURKEY RED LION INN

1. Preheat the oven to 450°.

2. Remove the neck, giblets, liver, etc. from the turkey. Use the liver in the stuffing. Set the rest aside. Rinse the turkey cavity well and pat dry.

3. Stuff the turkey with the Bread Stuffing, and truss the opening.

4. Place the turkey on a rack in a roasting pan. Rub the butter or margarine all over the skin. Combine the seasonings, and sprinkle them over the bird. Roast the turkey for 10 minutes. Reduce the heat to 350°, and roast for 20 to 25 minutes per pound, or until a meat thermometer registers 185°; this will take 3 ¹/₄ to 4 ¹/₄ hours. Baste often with the pan juices.

5. Meanwhile, if you like, cook all the turkey parts, except the livers for use later in the pan gravy. In a saucepan, cook the neck, giblets, heart, and gizzard over low heat, in water to cover, for 2 hours, until tender. Drain, remove the meat from the neck, and chop all the meats fine. Set aside to use in the gravy.

6. Remove the turkey from the oven and transfer it to a heated platter, reserving the pan juices. Let it rest, covered with foil, for 30 minutes.

7. Prepare the gravy. Remove the stuffing from the turkey and place it in a serving dish, keeping it warm until you are ready to use it. Carve the turkey and serve it with the stuffing and gravy.

Serves 10.

BREAD STUFFING

1. Preheat the oven to 350°. Butter a two-quart ovenproof casserole dish.

2. Melt ¹/₂ cup of the butter in a large saucepan. Add the vegetables and seasonings, and cook over medium heat, until tender, about 5 minutes.

3. Add the stock and bring it to a boil; boil gently for 30 minutes. Taste for seasonings, and add more salt and pepper, if desired. Remove the bay leaves.

4. If you plan to use the turkey livers, melt the remaining ¹/₄ cup butter in a sauté pan. Add the livers and sauté over medium heat until cooked through, about 5 minutes. Drain off the fat and chop the livers fine.

5. Place the bread cubes and the turkey livers (if desired) in a large bowl. Add 2 cups of the stock, with the vegetables, and mix well. Add the remaining stock ¹/₂ cup at a time, just until the bread is thoroughly moistened (the amount of stock used will depend on how dry the bread is).

6. Stuff the body and neck cavity of the turkey. Place the remaining stuffing in the prepared casserole and bake at 350° for 45 minutes, until golden brown on top.

Yields 8 to 10 cups.

³/₄ cup butter

1 onion, peeled and chopped

¹/₂ bunch celery, chopped

¹/₄ cup poultry seasoning

¹/₈ cup dried rubbed sage

4 bay leaves, whole

1 tablespoon garlic powder

1 tablespoon dried rosemary

dash salt and pepper

2 teaspoons dried thyme

3 to 4 cups turkey or chicken stock (*see page 38*)

20 slices day-old bread, cubed

turkey livers (optional)

PAN GRAVY

1. Skim the fat from the turkey pan juices. Strain, reserving the juices and the fat; you should have ¹/₄ cup of fat.

2. Heat the turkey fat in a saucepan. Add the flour and cook over low heat 5 to 8 minutes, until light golden in color, forming a roux. Add the reserved turkey juice and the stock to the roux. Using a wire whisk, whip until smooth. Add the seasonings and simmer for 30 minutes. Strain, and season with salt and pepper to taste. Add the chopped giblets, if desired.

Yields 2 cups.

¹/₄ cup flour

2 cups turkey or chicken stock (*see page 38*)

1 teaspoon dried savory

1 teaspoon dried rubbed sage

salt and pepper to taste

turkey giblets, cooked and chopped (optional)

4 beef tenderloin medallions (6 to 8 ounces each)

$^1/_2$ cup butter

$^1/_2$ cup lemon juice

$^1/_2$ cup parsley, chopped

salt and pepper to taste

SAUTÉED TENDERLOIN TIPS WITH LEMON BUTTER SAUCE

1. Slightly flatten the medallions, by pressing them lightly with the flat side of a French knife. Heat $^1/_4$ cup of the butter in a heavy skillet. When it is hot (but not burning) add the medallions and sauté them quickly — 3 minutes on one side and 2 minutes on the other. Place tenderloins on a warm platter.

2. Pour off all but 1 teaspoon fat from the pan. Add the remaining $^1/_4$ cup butter and the lemon juice. Scraping the pan, bring up all bits of the pan drippings. When the butter has melted, add the parsley and salt and pepper. Pour the sauce over the medallions, and serve immediately.

Serves 4.

Filet Mignon Red Lion Inn

1. Preheat the broiler.

2. Combine $^1/_4$ cup of the oil, Worcestershire sauce, and salt and pepper; blend well. Place the steaks in a small casserole or on a pie plate. Pour the oil mixture over them and marinate for 10 minutes, turning once. Drain, but reserve the marinade.

3. Transfer the steaks to the rack of a broiling pan and broil them for 6 to 8 minutes on the first side. Brush them with some of the marinade, turn them over, and broil for 6 minutes on other side (for medium rare).

4. Meanwhile, sauté the mushroom caps in a sauté pan over medium heat, in the remaining $^1/_4$ cup oil, until tender, about 5 minutes, and season them with salt and pepper. Remove them from the pan and keep them warm. In the same pan, sauté the bread to a golden brown.

5. Place each cooked steak on a piece of toast. Spoon some of the Béarnaise Sauce over the steak, and top with 2 mushroom caps. Serve immediately.

Serves 4.

$^1/_2$ cup vegetable oil

2 teaspoons Worcestershire sauce

salt and pepper to taste

4 center cuts filet mignon (6 to 8 ounces each)

4 slices white bread, crusts removed

8 mushroom caps, wiped clean

Béarnaise Sauce (*recipe below*)

Béarnaise Sauce

The addition of 1 teaspoon tomato paste to this Béarnaise Sauce will create a piquant and unusual Sauce Choron.

1. Combine all the ingredients except the Hollandaise Sauce in a saucepan, and bring to a boil. Reduce the heat and simmer until reduced to 2 to 4 tablespoons, about 15 minutes, being careful it does not burn or scorch.

2. Mix 2 tablespoons of the reduction into the Hollandaise Sauce, and serve. (Reserve the remainder of the reduction for another use. Cover and refrigerate for up to 3 months.)

Yields $^1/_2$ cup.

2 tablespoons shallots, finely chopped

1 teaspoon black peppercorns, crushed

1 tablespoon dried chervil

2 tablespoons dried tarragon

6 tablespoons red wine (burgundy is best)

3 tablespoons red wine vinegar

$^1/_2$ cup Hollandaise Sauce (*see page 82*)

1 corned beef brisket (4 to 5 pounds)

4 quarts chicken broth (*see page 38*)

1 teaspoon pickling spices

1 head garlic, cut in quarters (do not peel)

12 small new potatoes, scrubbed and peeled

6 carrots, peeled and cut into chunks

6 small turnips, peeled and diced

8 small beets, tops remaining

hot mustard (optional)

prepared horseradish sauce (optional)

New England Boiled Dinner

1. Place the corned beef and the broth in a Dutch oven. Add the pickling spices and garlic, and bring to a boil over high heat. Reduce the heat to low, cover, and simmer for 3 to 3 1/2 hours, until the beef is cooked.

2. Add the potatoes, carrots, and turnips to the pot, and cook for another 30 to 45 minutes, until the meat and vegetables are tender.

3. Meanwhile, cook the beets in a separate saucepan of boiling salted water for 30 to 45 minutes (this prevents them from discoloring the other vegetables).

4. Remove the beef and vegetables from their broth and arrange them on a heated serving platter. Pass the mustard and horseradish, if desired.

Serves 6 to 8.

SEAFOOD AND POULTRY

The abundance of cod, and its early popularity, are often mentioned when discussing New England food. This abundance is partly explained by Mrs. Isabella Beeton, in her 1861 book *Beeton's Book of Household Management*: "So extensive has been the consumption of this fish, that it is surprising that it has not long ago become extinct.... Yet it ceases to excite our wonder when we remember that the female can every year give birth to more than 9,000,000 [eggs] at a time."

Benjamin Franklin, who considered himself a confirmed vegetarian, could nevertheless be lured into eating cod, it appears, from the following description: "Being becalmed off Block Island, our people set about catching cod, and hauled up a great many. Hitherto I had stuck to my resolution of not eating animal food, and on this occasion I considered...the taking of every fish as a kind of unprovoked murder.... But I had formerly been a great lover of fish, and, when this came hot out of the frying-pan, it smelt admirably well. I balanced some time between principle and inclination, till I recollected that, when the fish were opened, I saw smaller fish taken out of their stomachs; then thought I, 'If you eat one another, I don't see why we mayn't eat you.' So I dined upon cod very heartily.... So convenient a thing it is to be a reasonable creature, since it enables one to find or make a reason for every thing one has a mind to do."

The abundance of salmon, especially in early summer, led to yet another New England tradition. Eastern salmon begin to "run" about the Fourth of July of each year, just as new vegetables are popping up in the garden. To celebrate, poached salmon with egg sauce, along with the first new potatoes and early peas, have become the traditional Fourth of July fare. The Red Lion Inn's recipe uses a Hollandaise in place of the egg sauce.

"The dining room is the heart and soul of a hotel. It must be agreeable in all its appointments. In color, in size, in outlook, in furnishing. The dining room at Plumb's [later The Red Lion Inn] invited entrance, inspired appetite; it was a pleasant place."

The Pittsfield Sun, September 3, 1896

³/₄ cup dry seasoned bread crumbs

1 ¹/₂ cups fresh crabmeat, flaked

³/₄ cup dry sherry

¹/₂ teaspoon lemon juice

4 fillets of sole (4 ounces each)

paprika

¹/₄ cup butter

FILLET OF SOLE WITH CRABMEAT STUFFING

1. Preheat the oven to 350°. Butter a baking dish large enough to hold the fillets in one layer.

2. Mix the bread crumbs, crabmeat, and sherry together in a bowl. Then add the lemon juice. The mixture should be moist but not wet.

3. Place one-fourth of the stuffing on each fillet, and roll the fillets up around the stuffing, keeping it tucked inside. Secure with a toothpick. Place the rolls in the prepared baking dish, seam side down. Sprinkle them lightly with paprika and dot each with 1 tablespoon butter.

4. Bake for 10 minutes at 350°, or until fish flakes when gently prodded with a fork. Serve immediately.

Serves 4.

FILLET OF SOLE VERONIQUE

1. Preheat oven to 325°. Butter an overproof baking dish large enough to hold the fillets in a single layer.

2. Melt the butter in a sauté pan. Add the flour and cook over medium heat until blended, about 2 to 3 minutes. Add 1 cup of the fish stock and cook over low heat, until reduced to $1/2$ cup. This will take about 30 to 45 minutes. Cool.

3. Roll up the fillets and place them in the prepared baking dish, seam side down. Cover the fillets completely with the remaining 1 cup fish stock and the white wine. Bake in a 325° oven for 8 to 10 minutes, until the fish flakes when gently prodded with a fork. Remove the pan from the oven and allow the fish to cool in the broth, about 15 minutes.

4. Preheat the broiler. Combine the Hollandaise Sauce and the whipped cream, folding them lightly together. Fold this into the reserved thickened fish stock.

5. Drain the poached fish and arrange it on a flameproof platter. Sprinkle with salt and pepper. Scatter the grapes over the fish and pour the sauce over all. Broil until delicately browned, about 3 to 5 minutes.

Serves 6.

2 tablespoons butter

3 tablespoons flour

2 cups fish stock

2 $1/2$ pounds fillet of sole

4 cups white wine

$2/3$ cup Hollandaise Sauce (*see page 82*)

$2/3$ cup cream, whipped

salt and pepper to taste

one bunch (about 30) green seedless grapes

24 large raw shrimp, shelled,
    cleaned, and deveined

2 eggs

1 tablespoon water

2 cups dried bread crumbs

$^1/_2$ cup Romano cheese, grated

1 teaspoon garlic powder

1 teaspoon dry mustard

salt and pepper to taste

$^1/_2$ cup butter

$^1/_4$ cup dry sherry

1 tablespoon lemon juice

SHRIMP MARIO

1. Beat the eggs and water together in a shallow bowl. In another shallow bowl, thoroughly mix the bread crumbs, cheese, garlic powder, mustard, salt, and pepper. Dip each shrimp first in the egg wash and then in the bread crumb mixture.

2. Melt the butter in a sauté pan and sauté the shrimp until they are lightly browned, about 2 to 3 minutes. At the last minute, add the sherry and lemon juice. (If the shrimp do not appear to be fully cooked at this point, place them in a baking dish and finish in a 350° oven for 5 minutes.)

3. Serve the shrimp on a hot platter, with the pan juices poured over them.

Serves 6.

POACHED FILLET OF SALMON

1. Prepare a bouquet garni by placing the celery, parsley, leek, bay leaves, and peppercorns on a square of cheesecloth, and tie it up to form a small bag.

2. Combine the fish stock or water, wine, pickling spices, lemon quarters, and bouquet garni in a stockpot and bring to a boil. Reduce the heat and simmer for 15 minutes.

3. Add the salmon to the broth, and poach over low heat until cooked, approximately 15 to 20 minutes, or until the fish flakes when gently prodded with a fork.

4. If you like, stir the dill into the Hollandaise Sauce.

5. Remove the salmon fillets from the broth, and arrange them on a warm serving platter. Top with the Hollandaise Sauce, and serve immediately.

Serves 4.

4 fillets of salmon (8 ounces each)

1 stalk celery, chopped

6 stalks parsley, chopped

1 leek, chopped (white part only)

2 bay leaves

12 black peppercorns

4 cups water or fish stock

3 cups white wine

$\frac{1}{4}$ cup pickling spices

2 lemons, quartered

1 cup Hollandaise Sauce (*see page 82*)

Fresh chopped dill (optional)

"(If) you like your dinner, man; never be ashamed to say so...remember that every man who has been worth a fig in this world, as poet, painter, or musician, has had a good appetite and a good taste."

William Makepeace Thackeray, Memorials of Gormandizing

SHRIMP SCAMPI

16 jumbo shrimp

16 clams

1 pound cooked angel hair or fettucini pasta

4 teaspoons olive oil

1 cup butter

2 tablespoons garlic, minced

1 cup white wine

2 teaspoons dried oregano

2 teaspoons dried basil

pinch of cayenne pepper

1. Peel the shrimp, leaving the tail section on. Split them along the back from tail to head, but do not slice clear through. Remove the vein, and rinse thoroughly.

2. Wash the clams thoroughly.

3. Cook the pasta in a pot of boiling, salted water, for 6 to 7 minutes if using angel hair or for 8 to 10 minutes if using fettucine. Drain thoroughly and toss with the olive oil in a large bowl. Keep warm.

4. Heat the butter in a large sauté pan, and add the garlic. Sauté lightly over medium low heat until soft and translucent. Add the shrimp, clams, wine, and seasonings. Cook until the shrimp are pink and the clams have opened, about 6 to 7 minutes. Discard any clams that do not open.

5. Serve the shrimp and clams over the hot pasta.

Serves 4.

Main Street, Stockbridge, in 1897, with The Red Lion Inn on the left.

CHICKEN WISCONSIN

1. Butter an ovenproof baking dish large enough to hold the chicken breasts in a single layer.

2. Melt $1/4$ cup of the butter in a sauté pan and sauté the minced onions over medium heat until translucent, but not browned, about 3 minutes. Add the mushrooms and sauté lightly, an additional 5 minutes. Add the salt, pepper and nutmeg, and cook for 1 additional minute. Remove from the heat and cool.

3. Mix the onion mixture, including the butter, into the softened cream cheese and blend well. Add the sherry and chill in the refrigerator until firm.

4. Preheat the oven to 425°. Split the chicken breasts in half. Laying each chicken breast skin side down on a flat surface, season with salt and pepper and place some of the cream cheese mixture in the middle of each. Roll the chicken breast, enclosing the cream cheese inside, and secure it with a toothpick. Season the outside of the breast with salt and pepper.

5. Place the chicken breasts in the prepared baking dish. In a small saucepan, melt the remaining $1/4$ cup of butter and add the wine to it, whisking them together well. Pour the mixture over the chicken. Bake at 425° for 40 minutes, until the chicken breasts are thoroughly cooked.

6. To serve, place two chicken breasts on each plate. Top with the Sauce Supreme and serve immediately.

Serves 4.

4 whole breasts of chicken, boned and skinned

4 teaspoons onions, minced

$1/2$ cup butter

4 teaspoons mushrooms, minced

salt and pepper to taste

$1/2$ teaspoon nutmeg

8 ounces cream cheese, softened to room temperature

4 teaspoons dry sherry

$1/4$ cup chablis, or other dry white wine

2 cups Sauce Supreme (*recipe follows*)

2 cups chicken stock (*see page 38*) or broth

2 tablespoons butter

2 tablespoons flour

salt and pepper to taste

$^1/_8$ teaspoon nutmeg

$^1/_4$ cup heavy cream

SAUCE SUPREME

1. In a medium saucepan, bring the chicken stock to a boil. Lower the heat and simmer until it is reduced to 1 cup, about 10 to 15 minutes.

2. In another saucepan, melt the butter and then add the flour, stirring to create a roux. Gently cook the roux for 4 to 5 minutes. Do not allow it to brown.

3. Whisk the reduced chicken stock into the butter and cook over medium heat for 5 to 6 minutes, until it is thickened. Add the seasonings and the cream. Heat for 1 minute only. Do not allow the sauce to boil at this point.

Yields 2 cups.

BAKED BOSTON SCROD

Scrod, a young cod, is strictly a New England dish, and abundantly available. It is firm, tender, and moist — a delightful fish.

1. Preheat the oven to 350°. Butter a baking pan large enough to hold the scrod in a single layer.

2. Place the scrod in the prepared baking pan, and add the salt, pepper, lemon juice, and wine. Drizzle 1/4 cup of the melted butter over the fish.

3. Bake at 350° for approximately 20 minutes, or until the fish flakes but is still moist. Remove the pan from the oven and preheat the broiler.

4. Scatter the bread crumbs over the fish, and drizzle with the remaining 1/4 cup butter. Brown under the broiler for 2 to 5 minutes only, until lightly browned, and serve.

Serves 4.

4 pieces scrod fillet (6 to 8 ounces each)

salt and pepper to taste

2 tablespoons lemon juice

1 1/2 cups white wine

1/2 cup butter, melted

1 cup dried bread crumbs

The cod was so important to Massachusetts economically that on March 17, 1784, the House of Representatives of the Commonwealth of Massachusetts voted to hang a representation of a cod in their chamber. Although it's been moved to new quarters several times since, it continues to hang in the current House chambers, as a perpetual reminder of the importance of the cod to the early welfare of the Commonwealth.

2 whole chicken breasts, boned and
  skinned

$^{1}/_{2}$ cup flour

salt and pepper to taste

$^{1}/_{2}$ cup milk

2 eggs

1 cup dried bread crumbs

1 cup sliced blanched almonds

$^{1}/_{4}$ cup vegetable oil

$^{1}/_{2}$ cup butter

1 cup Hollandaise Sauce (optional,
  see page 82)

CHICKEN BREAST ALMANDINE

1. Preheat the oven to 375°. Butter a baking dish large enough to hold the chicken breasts in a single layer.

2. Split the chicken breast into four pieces.

3. Mix the flour and salt and pepper together in a shallow dish. Beat the milk and eggs together in another shallow dish. Combine the bread crumbs and $^{1}/_{2}$ cup of the almonds in a third dish. Dip each chicken breast first in flour, then in the egg mixture, and finally in the bread crumbs.

4. Heat the oil and $^{1}/_{4}$ cup of the butter in a heavy skillet. Sauté the chicken over medium heat until golden brown, about 3 to 4 minutes on each side. Then transfer the chicken to the prepared baking dish and bake for 10 to 15 minutes in a 375° oven.

5. Sauté the remaining $^{1}/_{2}$ cup almonds in the remaining $^{1}/_{4}$ cup butter over low heat until lightly browned, about 5 minutes.

6. Serve the chicken breasts, topping them with Hollandaise Sauce if desired. Garnish with the almonds.

Serves 4.

FILLET OF SOLE WITH LOBSTER AND ASPARAGUS

At The Red Lion Inn, this dish is served with Wild and Brown Rice or Clam Rice Pilaf Red Lion Inn (*see pages 115 and 125*).

1. Melt the butter in a sauté pan, and add the lobster meat, asparagus, and white wine. Cook until the asparagus is just tender and the mixture is hot, about 3 to 5 minutes. Do not overcook. Season with salt and pepper to taste, and keep warm.

2. Season the flour with salt and pepper, and dredge the fillets in the flour.

3. Melt the clarified butter in another sauté pan, and sauté the fillets until golden, about 5 minutes on each side. Place the fish on a large platter, top with the asparagus and lobster, and cover with the Sauce Choron. Serve immediately.

Serves 4.

2 tablespoons butter

³/₄ pound cooked lobster meat, cut into chunks

16 asparagus spears

¹/₄ cup white wine

1 ¹/₂ pounds fillet of sole

¹/₂ cup flour

salt and pepper to taste

4 ¹/₂ tablespoons clarified butter (*see page 25*)

1 cup Sauce Choron (*recipe below*)

In 1622, when a group of new colonists arrived in Plymouth, Governor William Bradford was deeply humiliated because his colony was so short of food that the only "dish they could presente their friends with was a lobster...without bread or anything els but a cupp of fair water."

SAUCE CHORON

1. Heat the butter in a small saucepan, and add the tomatoes and tomato paste. Cook gently over low heat for 10 minutes until the juice has evaporated. Cool completely. Fold the tomatoes into the Hollandaise Sauce.

Yields 1 cup.

1 tablespoon butter

¹/₄ cup tomatoes, peeled, seeded, and minced very fine

¹/₂ teaspoon tomato paste

³/₄ cup Hollandaise Sauce (*see page 82*)

20 jumbo shrimp

2 ¹/₄ cups Shrimp Stuffing (*recipe follows*)

¹/₄ cup butter, melted

3 tablespoons white wine

paprika

2 cups hot cooked white rice

1 cup White Wine Sauce (*recipe below*)

BAKED JUMBO SHRIMP

1. Preheat the oven to 350°. Butter a baking dish large enough to hold the shrimp in a single layer.

2. Peel the shrimp, leaving the tail section on. Split them along the back from tail to head, but do not slice clear through. Remove the vein, and rinse thoroughly.

3. Place 2 tablespoons of the stuffing into the cavity along the back of each shrimp, and arrange them in the prepared baking dish. Pour the melted butter and white wine over them, and then sprinkle with paprika.

4. Bake at 350° for 15 to 20 minutes, until the shrimp are pink and cooked through.

5. Place some cooked rice on each plate, and arrange the shrimp on top. Cover with the White Wine Sauce, and serve.

Serves 4.

2 tablespoons shallots, chopped

8 tablespoons butter

¹/₄ cup chablis or other white wine

1 cup heavy cream

pinch cayenne pepper

salt and pepper to taste

WHITE WINE SAUCE

1. Heat 2 tablespoons of the butter in a small skillet, and sauté the shallots over medium heat until soft, about 3 to 5 minutes. Add the wine and cook over medium heat until the pan is almost dry, about 5 to 10 minutes. Then add the cream and reduce the mixture again until it is thick and creamy, about 6 to 8 minutes. Season with cayenne, salt, and pepper. Slowly swirl in the remaining 6 tablespoons butter. Do not boil.

Yields 1 cup.

SHRIMP STUFFING

This stuffing is also excellent when used with a fillet of sole.

1. Heat the butter in a skillet, and sauté the shallots and celery over medium heat until translucent, about 5 minutes. Add the seafood and sauté for 2 minutes, or until just cooked.

2. Add the bread crumbs and seasonings and sauté for 2 minutes. Then stir in the sherry and parsley, and remove from the heat. When the mixture is cool, stir in the egg. Stuffing not used for the shrimp can be baked in a buttered baking dish for 30 minutes in a 350° oven, and served on the side.

Yields 4 cups.

$1/2$ cup butter

2 tablespoons shallots, minced

3 stalks celery, diced

$1/2$ pound baby shrimp, whole

$1/2$ pound white fish (haddock, cod, sole, etc.), cubed

$1/2$ pound scallops, halved

1 $1/2$ cups dried bread crumbs

salt and pepper to taste

1 teaspoon paprika

1 teaspoon dried thyme

$1/8$ teaspoon cayenne pepper

2 tablespoons dry sherry

$1/4$ cup parsley, chopped

1 egg, beaten

3 tablespoons olive oil

1 cup onion, coarsely chopped

1 cup green pepper, coarsely chopped

1 tablespoon garlic, crushed

2 cups fish stock or canned clam juice

1 cup tomatoes, peeled, seeded, and coarsely chopped

$^1/_2$ cup dry white wine

2 tablespoons parsley, finely chopped

1 bay leaf

salt and pepper to taste

4 soft shell crabs (or 2 Dungeness crabs)

8 to 12 mussels in the shell

8 to 12 clams in the shell

4 to 8 large shrimp, shelled and deveined

$^3/_4$ pound cod, halibut, sea bass, or any combination of firm-fleshed white fish, cubed

dash dry sherry

CIOPPINO

1. Heat the olive oil in a 2- or 3-quart enameled pot over moderate heat until a light haze forms, about 5 minutes. Add the onions, green peppers, and garlic. Cook for about 5 minutes, stirring frequently until the onions are soft and translucent, but not brown.

2. Stir in the fish stock, tomatoes, wine, parsley, and bay leaf. Bring to a boil, reduce the heat, and partially cover. Simmer for 30 minutes. Then add the salt and pepper, and remove the bay leaf.

3. To assemble the cioppino, arrange the crabs in the bottom of a 3- to 5-quart casserole or skillet. Lay the mussels, clams, shrimp, and fish on top and pour the tomato mixture over all.

4. Bring to a boil, reduce the heat to low, and cook for 5 to 10 minutes. The cioppino is done when the mussel and clam shells have opened and the fish flakes easily when prodded gently with a fork. Discard any mussels or clams that remain closed.

5. Serve at once, directly from the casserole; or spoon the fish and shellfish into a large heated tureen, pour the tomato mixture over them, and serve, adding a dash of sherry just before serving.

Serves 4.

SOLE ALMANDINE

1. Heat $^1/_4$ cup of the butter in a medium skillet, and sauté the almonds over low heat, just until browned, about 5 minutes. Remove them from the pan and set aside

2. Season the flour with salt and pepper, and dredge the fillets in the flour.

3. Melt the remaining $^1/_2$ cup butter in the skillet. Sauté the sole over medium heat on both sides until it flakes easily when prodded with a fork, approximately 2 to 3 minutes on each side.

4. Transfer the fish to a heated platter, and top with the Hollandaise Sauce. Sprinkle with the almonds and serve immediately.

Serves 4.

$^3/_4$ cup butter

$^1/_2$ cup sliced blanched almonds

1 cup flour

salt and pepper to taste

8 pieces fillet of sole (3 to 4 ounces each)

1 cup Hollandaise Sauce (*see page 82*)

LINCOLN RUSSELL

The Jean Dewey Suite in The O'Brien House, one of the separate cottages on the Red Lion Inn property.

4 whole chicken breasts, boned
and skinned

salt and pepper to taste

3 tablespoons butter

2 tablespoons shallots, finely
chopped

$^1/_2$ cup white wine

$^1/_2$ cup chicken stock (*see page 38*)
or broth

2 sprigs fresh parsley

2 packages (10 ounces each) fresh
spinach, stemmed and well
rinsed

2 tablespoons flour

1 cup heavy cream

1 egg yolk, lightly beaten

2 tablespoons Parmesan cheese, or
to taste

CHICKEN BREASTS FLORENTINE

1. Lay the chicken breasts on flat surface, and sprinkle them with salt and pepper. Roll up the chicken breasts and secure them with a toothpick.

2. Grease the bottom of a skillet with 1 tablespoon of the butter, and sprinkle with the shallots. Arrange the chicken breasts, seam side down, in the skillet. Add the wine, chicken stock, salt and pepper, and parsley. Bring to a boil, cover, and simmer for about 20 minutes, until the chicken is just cooked.

3. Drain and reserve all liquid from the chicken breasts; there should be about 1 $^1/_2$ cups. Remove the toothpick, cover the chicken breasts and keep them warm.

4. Cook the spinach leaves in a large saucepan over medium heat, in just enough water to cover for approximately 5 minutes, or until wilted. Drain well, pressing to remove excess water.

5. Preheat the broiler. Melt the remaining 2 tablespoons butter in a saucepan and add the flour, stirring with a wire whisk until blended, about 2 to 3 minutes. Add the reserved chicken cooking liquid, stirring until blended. When the mixture is smooth, simmer for about 5 minutes until thickened. Add the cream, and cook an additional 2 minutes. Remove the pan from the heat. Allow to cool for 5 minutes, then spoon $^1/_2$ cup of the sauce into the egg yolk, return it to the pan, and stir briskly.

6. Spoon the spinach onto the center of a flameproof serving dish. Arrange the chicken breasts, seam side down, over the spinach. Spoon the sauce over the chicken and spinach and sprinkle with the cheese. Broil until bubbly and golden on top, about 5 minutes.

Serves 4.

SCALLOPS AND MUSHROOMS

Chef Mongeon sometimes serves these scallops in a prepared puff pastry shell.

1. Heat $^1/_4$ cup of the butter in a skillet, and sauté the onions and mushrooms over medium heat until the onions are translucent. Add the sherry and scallops, and cook until the scallops turn white, about 8 minutes. Strain, reserving the liquid. Keep the scallops and vegetables warm.

2. Melt the remaining $^1/_4$ cup butter in another skillet, and add the flour to form a roux. Cook for 2 to 3 minutes over medium heat. Cool slightly.

3. Scald the cream in a small saucepan and add it gradually to the flour mixture. Cook over low heat, stirring, until thickened, about 10 minutes. Add the reserved scallop liquid. Add cayenne, salt, and pepper.

4. Combine the scallops and the vegetables with the sauce, and gently reheat. Serve immediately.

Serves 4.

$^1/_2$ cup butter

1 medium onion, finely diced

$^1/_2$ pound mushrooms, sliced

2 tablespoons dry sherry

1 pound fresh scallops

$^1/_4$ cup flour

1 cup heavy cream

cayenne pepper to taste

salt and white pepper to taste

VEGETABLES, RICE, AND POTATOES

Early New Englanders lived off the bounty of the land and grew an abundance of vegetables, fruit, berries, and grains. Fresh vegetables were always preferred, but when the supply was overly abundant, vegetables were stewed, or made into a sauce — which frugal Pilgrim housewives called garden sass. These sauces were poured over meat and fish, to give them variety.

From the surviving letters of John and Abigail Adams, we learn about the trials of early farm life in Massachusetts. Abigail was often left with the duties of running the farm, while John attended to his duties as vice president or president of the new United States. Yet it was John who always voiced a preference for "the Delights of a Garden to the Dominion of a World." Even after moving to Washington, Abigail made sure John was regularly provided with the "fresh russet potatoes" and the "sweet apples from our tree."

Corn, squash, and beans are generally mentioned as the first New England vegetables, and they remain popular today. Corn was used in a variety of ways, but it was often thought ill-mannered to eat it directly from the cob, as the following note from *The American Heritage Cookbook* indicates: "Some people take the whole stem," Fredrika Bremer wrote on her visit to America in 1850, "and gnaw [the kernels] out with their teeth: two gentlemen do so who sit opposite...myself at table, and who we call 'the sharks.'"

Owners of The Red Lion Inn often maintained a garden in back from which they supplied their tables with fresh vegetables. According to an unsigned letter in The Red Lion Inn scrapbook dated November 8, 1929 (when the Plumbs owned the inn), "The owner had a garden where early vegetables were grown and were then, as now, a great luxury to the city visitors."

Although there is currently no garden in back of the inn, Milton Bass wrote in a 1973 *Berkshire Eagle* article that "Mrs. Fitzpatrick is still farm girl enough to be happiest with fresh rather than frozen or canned." This preference for "fresh" is reflected in the following recipes.

"It is not elegant to gnaw Indian corn. The kernels should be scored with a knife, scraped off into the plate, and then eaten with a fork. Ladies should be particularly careful how they manage so ticklish a dainty, lest the exhibition rub off a little desirable romance."

Hints on Etiquette, 1844

RED LION INN WILD AND BROWN RICE

1. Melt the butter in a deep saucepan. Add the chopped vegetables and the seasonings. Sauté for 7 minutes over medium heat until the vegetables are wilted. Remove the bay leaf.

2. Add the beef stock and bring to a boil. Add both rices, stir, and cover. Cook for 50 to 60 minutes over medium heat, stirring frequently, until the rice is tender and it has absorbed the stock.

Serves 8.

$^1/_2$ cup butter

$^3/_4$ cup onion, chopped

1 $^1/_2$ cups celery, chopped

$^1/_4$ cup dried marjoram

2 tablespoons garlic powder

dash of salt and pepper

2 bay leaves

5 cups beef stock (*see page 37*) or broth

1 cup brown rice

1 cup wild rice

RED LION INN RICE

1. Melt the butter in a saucepan. Add the vegetables and seasonings, and sauté for 7 minutes over medium heat until the vegetables are wilted. Remove the bay leaves.

2. Add the chicken stock and bring to a boil. Stir in the rice, cover, and cook over medium heat for 30 to 45 minutes, stirring frequently, until the rice is tender and it has absorbed the stock.

Serves 8.

$^1/_2$ cup butter

2 stalks celery, finely chopped

$^1/_2$ onion, peeled and finely chopped

$^1/_2$ pound mushrooms, wiped clean and finely chopped

2 tablespoons garlic powder

2 teaspoons dried thyme

2 bay leaves

dash of salt and pepper

4 cups chicken stock (*see page 38*) or broth

2 cups white rice

6 to 8 large yams or sweet potatoes

$1/4$ cup dark corn syrup

$1/4$ cup light corn syrup

1/4 cup light brown sugar

2 tablespoons maple syrup

$1/4$ cup Kentucky bourbon

chopped parsley, for garnish

Candied Yams with Bourbon

1. Preheat the oven to 350°. Butter an 8" square baking dish.

2. In a large pot filled with enough water to cover the sweet potatoes or yams, boil them just until tender, about 45 minutes. Peel them while they are still hot. Slice the potatoes lengthwise and then crosswise, and allow them to cool. Arrange them in the prepared casserole.

3. Combine the remaining ingredients except the parsley, and pour them over the potatoes. Bake them at 350° for 30 minutes or until bubbling hot. Garnish with fresh chopped parsley and serve.

Serves 10 to 12.

3 pounds butternut squash, peeled, seeded, and coarsely chopped

$1/2$ cup butter

$1/4$ cup light brown sugar

2 tablespoons maple syrup

1 teaspoon salt

$1/2$ teaspoon white pepper

$1/2$ teaspoon nutmeg

Fresh parsley, chopped

Red Lion Inn Whipped Butternut Squash

1. Preheat the oven to 350°. Butter a 3-quart baking dish.

2. Boil the squash in salted water to cover, until tender, about 20 minutes, and drain well. While it is still hot, combine the squash with the remaining ingredients (except the parsley) in a mixing bowl, and whip with a beater until smooth. Taste and adjust the seasonings.

3. Spoon the squash into the prepared baking dish, cover, and bake for 10 to 15 minutes, or until piping hot. Sprinkle with the chopped parsley, and serve.

Serves 10 to 12.

Baked Jumbo Shrimp, page 108.

Hors d'oeuvre and wine in front of the lobby fireplace.

Champagne breakfast in a Red Lion Inn room,
featuring Eggs Benedict with Canadian Bacon, page 186.

Chicken Wisconsin, page 103, on the Red Lion Inn's traditional Blue Willow china.

Chocolate Covered Strawberries, page 159.

The Lion's Den, The Red Lion Inn's pub, with light fare and nightly entertainment.

Baked Stuffed Tomato with Rice, Saffron, and Peas, page 122.

Dinner in the Main Dining Room.

Challah, page 76.

Duck Salad with Strawberry Vinaigrette, page 47.

New England Clam Chowder,
page 31.

Vegetable Bundles, page 119.

Escargots Red Lion in Puff Pastry Shells, page 19.

Indian Pudding, hot from the Red Lion's oven, page 142.

A melange of Red Lion Inn breads, from top right clockwise. Cheese Bread, page 65; Apple Cider Bread, page 73. On plate: Cranberry Orange Nut Bread, page 68; and Apricot Nut Bread, page 72. Red Lion Inn Lemon Bread, page 67; French Bread, page 70; Clover Leaf Cheese Rolls, page 65. On the pewter plate in center: Blueberry Muffins, page 66; Knotted French Rolls, page 70; Pumpkin Muffins, page 64; and Mike's Bran Muffins, page 71.

New England Salmon Cakes with Creamy Celery Sauce, page 173.

Blackberry Tansey, page 147.

Bloody Mary, page 193.

Corn Fritters, page 169, and Red Lion Inn Breakfast Sausage, page 182, served in The Widow Bingham's Tavern.

Sirloin of Venison with Red Wine Sauce, page 80, with Red Lion Inn Wild and Brown Rice, page 115.

Chocolate Chip Pie with Hot Fudge Sauce, page 134.

Cheesecake with New England Blueberry Sauce, page 137.

Roast Christmas Goose with Orange Gravy and Apple Apricot Chestnut Dressing, pages 87 through 89.

CREAMED ONIONS

1. Boil the onions in salted water to cover until tender, about 30 minutes. Drain well.

2. Bring the milk to a boil in a small saucepan. Melt the butter in another saucepan, add the flour to the butter and cook over low heat for 2 minutes. Do not brown. Whisk in the hot milk and continue whisking until the sauce is smooth, then add the cloved onion, bay leaf, nutmeg, salt, pepper, and mace. Simmer for 20 minutes. Strain.

3. Add the onions to the cream sauce and reheat. Add salt and pepper if desired, garnish with the chives, and serve.

Serves 6.

20 small white onions, about 3 pounds, peeled

2 cups milk

$1/4$ cup butter

$1/4$ cup flour

1 small onion, studded with 3 whole cloves

1 bay leaf

$1/8$ teaspoon nutmeg

salt and pepper to taste

dash ground mace

salt and pepper to taste

$1/4$ cup chives, minced

8 baking potatoes

4 teaspoons vegetable oil

$^1/_2$ cup milk, heated

10 tablespoons butter

2 tablespoons sour cream

1 $^1/_4$ teaspoons salt

$^1/_4$ teaspoon pepper

3 tablespoons dried chives

2 tablespoons Dijon-style mustard

$^1/_4$ cup Parmesan cheese, grated

$^1/_4$ cup bacon bits

paprika

BAKED STUFFED POTATOES RED LION

1. Preheat the oven to 350°.

2. Wash the potatoes well. Rub the skins with the oil, and prick them twice with a fork. Bake at 350° for 1 hour.

3. Cut the tops off the potatoes while they still very hot. Scoop out the potato pulp (be careful not to pierce the skin) and combine it with the hot milk, 5 tablespoons of the butter, the sour cream, salt and pepper, chives, and mustard. Whip until smooth.

4. Place the whipped potatoes in a pastry bag fitted with a star tip and pipe the filling back into potato shells. Sprinkle with the Parmesan cheese and bacon bits and dust with paprika. Melt the remaining 5 tablespoons butter and drizzle it over the potatoes.

5. Bake at 350° for 10 minutes, until the tops are golden crisp.

Serves 8.

"Nor do I say, that it is filthy to eat potatoes. I do not ridicule the using of them as sauce. What I laugh at is, the idea of the use of them...in lieu of wheat.... As food for cattle, sheep or hogs, this is the worst of all the green and root crops; but of this I have said enough before; and therefore, I now dismiss the Potato with the hope, that I shall never again have to write the word, or see the thing."

William Cobbett, A Year's Residence in the United States of America, 1819

VEGETABLE BUNDLES

1. Preheat the oven to 350°. Butter a 3-quart ovenproof casserole dish.

2. Trim the asparagus to 2 $\frac{1}{2}$" in length, and peel off any outside woody spots.

3. Combine all the vegetables, except the leek tops, in a steamer, and steam until tender, but still firm.

4. Cut the damaged ends off the leek tops, then cut the remaining leaves into strips about 8" long and about $\frac{1}{8}$" wide. Rinse them thoroughly and put them in a saucepan with water to cover. Cook over medium heat for 1 minute. Drain, and plunge them into cold water to stop the cooking.

5. Using one piece of each vegetable, hold them together and tie in the middle with a piece of leek, finishing with a bow.

6. Arrange the bundles in the prepared casserole, and top each bundle with salt, pepper, and 1 teaspoon melted butter. Pour the wine over the vegetables, and bake at 350° for 10 to 12 minutes. Serve immediately.

Serves 8.

16 fresh asparagus spears, medium size

16 carrots, cut into julienne strips

16 red bell peppers, cut into julienne strips

8 leeks, tops only

salt and pepper

3 tablespoons butter, melted

4 teaspoons white wine

2 pounds medium-sized white potatoes, peeled

6 cups water

8 tablespoons butter

6 ounces hickory-smoked ham, diced

1 cup onion, minced

$^1/_3$ cup heavy cream, heated

salt and pepper to taste

$^1/_4$ cup Parmesan cheese, grated

RED LION POTATOES

If any of these potatoes are left over, Chef Mongeon suggests forming them into patties and sautéing them in butter.

1. Preheat the oven to 375°. Butter an 8" square casserole dish.

2. Bring the water to a boil, add the potatoes, and cook until tender (30 to 40 minutes). Drain, but keep hot.

3. Heat 4 tablespoons of the butter in a skillet, and sauté the ham and onions over medium heat, just until the onions are translucent, about 5 minutes. Drain, reserving the cooking juices.

4. Place the potatoes in the bowl of an electric mixer, fitted with a whip. Add 3 tablespoons of the remaining butter, the hot cream, the cooking juices from the ham and onions, salt and pepper, and half of the Parmesan cheese. Whip until the potatoes are smooth. Add the ham and onions. Adjust seasonings to taste.

5. Place the potatoes in the prepared casserole dish. Dot with the remaining 1 tablespoon butter, and sprinkle with the remaining cheese. Bake in a 375° oven until bubbly hot and golden (about 20 to 25 minutes).

Serves 6 to 8.

"Potatoes will clean linen as well as soap."

Mrs. Isabella Beeton, Beeton's Book of Household Management, 1861

CHANTILLY POTATOES

1. Bring the water to a boil, add the potatoes, and cook until tender, about 30 to 40 minutes. Drain well, but keep hot.

2. Place the potatoes in the bowl of an electric mixer fitted with a whip, and beat them on low speed. Add the butter, salt, and hot cream, and whip until smooth. Then add the sour cream, onion powder, peppers, and chives. Whip quickly to incorporate. Check for seasonings. Serve piping hot.

Serves 6 to 8.

2 pounds medium-sized potatoes, peeled

6 cups boiling water

$^1/_4$ cup butter

$^1/_2$ teaspoon salt

$^1/_3$ cup heavy cream, heated

3 tablespoons sour cream

1 teaspoon onion powder

white pepper to taste

cayenne pepper to taste

$^1/_4$ cup chives, minced

GLAZED CARROTS WITH GRAPES

1. Cut the carrots lengthwise into thin julienne strips. Bring the water to a boil, add salt, and cook the carrots just until tender, 8 to 10 minutes. Drain, and set aside.

2. Cut the grapes in half.

3. Melt the butter in a skillet, add the brown sugar and carrots, and sauté over medium heat for 2 minutes. Then add the grapes, salt, pepper, and nutmeg, and sauté 2 minutes more.

4. Serve piping hot, sprinkling each serving with chopped parsley.

Serves 6 to 8.

1 pound carrots, peeled

5 cups water

60 to 80 seedless green grapes (10 per serving)

$^1/_2$ cup butter

2 tablespoons light brown sugar

salt and pepper to taste

pinch ground nutmeg

1 tablespoon parsley, chopped

6 medium-sized tomatoes

¹/₄ cup butter

¹/₂ cup onion, peeled and diced

1 cup white rice

¹/₂ cup chablis

1/8 teaspoon saffron

1 ¹/₂ cups chicken stock (*see page 38*) or broth

salt and pepper to taste

pinch cayenne pepper

¹/₂ cup frozen peas

¹/₂ cup pimiento, minced

2 tablespoon parsley, chopped

BAKED STUFFED TOMATOES WITH RICE, SAFFRON, AND PEAS

1. Preheat the oven to 375°. Butter a shallow ovenproof dish large enough to hold 12 tomatoes.

2. Rinse the tomatoes, and cut them in half horizontally. Cut a thin slice off the bottom of each tomato so it will sit flat. Squeeze or scoop out the seeds and pulp, leaving a shell.

3. Melt the butter in a skillet, and sauté the onions over medium heat until they are translucent, about 5 minutes. Do not let them brown. Add the rice and sauté over low heat for 2 minutes to coat with butter; do not brown. Add the chablis and saffron, and cook for 3 minutes, stirring constantly. Then add the chicken stock and bring to a boil. Cover, and cook until the rice has absorbed all the liquid, about 30 minutes. Allow the mixture to cool about 5 minutes. Season with salt, pepper, and cayenne. Fold in the frozen peas, pimiento, and parsley.

4. Stuff the tomatoes with the rice mixture, and arrange them in the prepared baking dish. Bake in a 375° oven for 15 minutes, or until the rice is hot and the tomatoes have softened slightly.

Serves 12.

RISSOLE POTATOES WITH ROSEMARY AND GARLIC

1. Preheat the oven to 375°.

2. Remove a ring of peel from around the circumference of each potato. Soak the potatoes in cold water to cover to prevent discoloring until you are ready to use them.

3. Heat the oil and butter in a sauté pan, add the rosemary and garlic, and sauté over low heat for 5 to 6 minutes, until the herbs have perfumed the oil, but have not browned.

4. Remove the herbs from the flavored oil and add the potatoes to the skillet. Sauté the potatoes over medium heat until golden, about 10 minutes.

5. Place the potatoes in a roasting pan, sprinkle them with salt and pepper, and bake them in a 375° oven until tender, about 40 to 50 minutes. Sprinkle them with the chopped parsley just before serving.

Serves 6.

12 Red Bliss potatoes

6 tablespoons olive oil

6 tablespoons butter

2 tablespoons dried rosemary

2 cloves garlic, cut in half

salt and pepper to taste

2 tablespoons parsley, chopped

Interior of the Red Lion's restored Victorian elevator cage.

CLEMENS KALISCHER

1 pound zucchini

24 cherry tomatoes

1 bunch fresh basil leaves (about 24)

$^{1}/_{4}$ cup olive oil

2 cloves garlic, chopped

salt and pepper to taste

pinch cayenne pepper

$^{1}/_{4}$ cup Parmesan cheese, grated (optional)

SAUTÉED ZUCCHINI WITH CHERRY TOMATOES AND BASIL

1. Wash the zucchini and trim the ends. Slice them very thin.

2. Rinse the cherry tomatoes, and cut them in half.

3. Rinse the basil leaves, making sure there is no sand in them. Save the best leaves (about half) for garnish. Chop the remaining leaves.

4. Heat the olive oil and chopped garlic in a skillet or wok over low heat for 3 minutes; do not brown. Add the zucchini and sauté, stirring, for 2 to 3 minutes. Add the cherry tomatoes, and stir fry 2 to 3 minutes. Add chopped basil and cayenne pepper. Cook an additional 2 minutes. Adjust the seasonings to your taste.

5. Place the zucchini on a platter, and garnish with the whole basil leaves. Serve with a sprinkling of Parmesan cheese, if desired.

Serves 6 to 8.

"The cherry tomato is a marvelous invention, producing as it does a satisfactorily explosive squish when bitten."

Miss Manners

CLAM RICE PILAF

Chef Mongeon likes to serve this rice as a side accompaniment to fish dishes. If you are using it as a side dish for roast chicken or a game hen, substitute chicken stock for the clam broth, or if you are serving it with beef, beef broth can be substituted.

1. Melt 4 tablespoons of the butter in a heavy skillet. Add the onions and sauté over medium heat until they are wilted, about 5 minutes. Remove the onions, and set them aside.

2. Add the pasta to the skillet and sauté for 2 minutes, until golden brown. Add the rice and stir well. Then add the white wine, reserved onions, and bay leaves.

3. Add clam broth and bring to a boil. Cover, reduce the heat to a simmer, and cook for 25 to 30 minutes, or until all the liquid has been absorbed. Remove the skillet from the heat and set it aside, covered, for 5 minutes.

4. Fluff the rice with a fork. Add salt and pepper, the parsley, and the remaining 4 tablespoons butter. Serve.

Serves 8 to 10.

8 tablespoons unsalted butter

$1/4$ cup onions, peeled and minced

$1/2$ cup fresh angel hair pasta

2 cups long grain white rice

4 cups fresh or bottled clam broth

$1/4$ cup white wine

2 bay leaves

salt and pepper to taste

3 tablespoons chopped parsley

Pies and Cakes

Americans love desserts, especially pies and cakes. Apple pie was such a staple of early American cooking that it was eaten for breakfast, lunch, dinner, and supper.

It is said that the first orchards in New England were planted by William Blaxton, a clergyman who owned, for a time, a farm on Beacon Hill in Boston. He moved to Rhode Island in 1635 and raised what is now called the Sweet Rhode Island Greening — the first variety of apple to be grown in the United States.

Perhaps those first apple pies were not the melt-in-your-mouth types we love today, however, for a Dr. Acrelius wrote in 1758, "House-pie, in country places, is made of apples neither peeled nor freed from their cores, and its crust is not broken if a wagon wheel goes over it."

By 1851, however, American housewives had learned a thing or two, because we have a new assessment from an immigrant living in Wisconsin, who wrote to friends in Norway, "Strawberries, raspberries, and blackberries thrive here. From these they make a wonderful dish combined with syrup and sugar, which is called pai. I can tell you that is something that glides easily down your throat; they also make the same sort of pai out of apples or finely ground meat, with syrup added, and that is really the most superb."

As much as early settlers loved pies, however, one pie apparently came into disfavor shortly after the settlers arrived. Mince pie at Christmas had been popular in England long before there was an America, but it was banned in Boston because it was traditionally baked in a dish shaped to symbolize the Christ Child's manger, with the spices representing the gifts of the Wise Men. Puritans considered it an idolatrous horror and prohibited its making.

It's a good thing that most households had a few chickens to produce eggs for the family, because they were used prodigiously. Amelia Simmons in her 1796 book *American Cookery* gives a cake recipe calling for twenty pounds of flour, fifteen pounds of sugar, ten pounds of butter, and four dozen eggs. Mrs. Chadwick in *Home Cookery* includes a cake recipe that calls for ninety eggs, plus the whites of nineteen more for the frosting. Although these were wedding cakes, an ordinary one might ask for the yolks of thirty-two eggs.

Due to large family sizes, and frequent dinner guests, pies were also made in enormous quantities. Harriet Beecher Stowe wrote in her book *Oldtown Folks, A Story of New England* that Thanksgiving pies were made in "forties, fifties, and hundreds" and made of "everything in the earth and under the earth... pumpkins, cranberries, huckleberries, cherries, green currants, peaches, pears, plums, custards, apples...pies with top crusts and pies without, pies adorned with all sorts of fanciful fluting and architectural strips...."

Chocolate cake holds a festive place in most American kitchens, too, and since chocolate was first imported by a New Englander, it's especially popular in this region. In 1765 Dr. James Baker of Dorchester, Massachusetts, financed the first chocolate mill in America. Baker imported the cocoa beans from the West Indies, and a new industry was born.

The Red Lion Inn is justifiably noted for its desserts, including apple pie and chocolate cake. Some of the recipes have been handed down from generation to generation, while others are relatively new to the Red Lion Inn repertoire.

"Pumpkin pie," according to The House Mother, *"if rightly made, is a thing of beauty and a joy — while it lasts.... Pies that cut a little less firm than a pine board, and those that run round your plate are alike to be avoided. Two inches deep is better than the thin plates one sometimes sees, that look for all the world like pumpkin flap-jacks.... With the pastry light, tender, and not too rich, and a generous filling of smooth spiced sweetness — a little 'trembly' as to consistency, and delicately brown on top — a perfect pumpkin pie, eaten before the life has gone out of it, is one of the real additions made by American cookery to the good things of the world."*

The American Heritage Cookbook

5 pounds McIntosh apples, peeled, cored, and sliced (if McIntosh are not available, substitute another tart apple such as Cortland)

1 cup plus 1 tablespoon sugar

2 teaspoon ground cinnamon

crust for a two-crust pie (*recipe follows*)

1 tablespoon butter

1 egg

1 tablespoon milk

"But I, when I undress me
Each night, upon my knees
Will ask the Lord to bless me
With apple-pie and cheese."

Eugene Field (1850-1895), Apple-Pie and Cheese

RED LION INN APPLE PIE

President Calvin Coolidge said he never ate anything half as good as the pork apple pies his stepmother made. One hopes he and Mrs. Coolidge tried the Red Lion Inn apple pie on one of their visits. We bet it's every bit as good as his Mom's.

1. Preheat the oven to 375°.

2. Place the apples in a large bowl. Combine 1 cup of the sugar and the cinnamon, and add to the apples. Toss until well mixed.

3. Fill the unbaked pie shell with the apple mixture, and dot with the butter. Fit the top crust over the filling, and crimp the top and bottom edges together to seal the apples in.

4. Whisk together the egg and the milk. Brush the top crust with this egg wash, and sprinkle with the remaining 1 tablespoon sugar. Pierce the top crust in several places with a sharp knife.

5. Bake at 375° for 50 to 60 minutes, or until the apples are tender when tested with a thin knife.

Yields 1 pie.

PIE CRUST FOR TWO-CRUST PIE

$^1/_2$ cup butter, cold

$^1/_2$ cup shortening

2 $^1/_4$ cups flour

$^3/_4$ teaspoon salt

$^1/_2$ cup milk, cold

1. Blend the butter and shortening together with a wooden spoon in a small bowl.

2. Sift the flour and salt together into a large bowl. Cut in the butter and shortening, using a pastry blender or two knives, until the mixture resembles cornmeal. Add the cold milk, and blend until absorbed. Divide the dough in half and roll each half into a ball. Wrap them in plastic wrap and refrigerate until chilled, about 30 minutes. (Or, if using a food processor, place the butter, shortening, flour, and salt in the bowl; fit with a steel blade. Process until the mixture reaches the consistency of cornmeal. With the processor on, add the milk slowly through the funnel until the dough forms a ball.)

3. When you are ready to bake the pie, roll each half of the chilled pie dough out on a floured board until it is slightly larger than the pie plate. Fit one half into the pie plate, place a filling inside, add the top crust, and flute the edges together.

Yields 2 crusts.

2 cups vegetable oil

2 ²/₃ cups sugar

6 eggs

1 teaspoon vanilla

2 ²/₃ cups flour

2 ¹/₂ teaspoons baking powder

4 ¹/₂ teaspoons baking soda

¹/₂ teaspoon salt

2 teaspoons ground cinnamon

2 ²/₃ cups carrots, grated

4 cups canned crushed pineapple,
     well drained

1 ³/₄ cups walnuts, chopped

Cream Cheese Frosting (*recipe
     below*)

¹/₄ cup butter, softened

¹/₄ cup cream cheese, softened

1 pound confectioners' sugar

1 teaspoon vanilla

2 to 4 tablespoons milk

CARROT CAKE

1. Preheat the oven to 350°. Grease and flour two 9" round cake pans.

2. Cream the oil and sugar together well in a large bowl. Add the eggs, one at a time, mixing well after each. Add the vanilla, and cream well.

3. Sift the flour, baking powder, baking soda, salt, and cinnamon together. Add to the creamed mixture, and mix with an electric mixer for about 5 minutes. Stir in the carrots, pineapple, and walnuts.

4. Pour the batter into the prepared cake pans, and bake at 350° for 40 to 45 minutes, until a cake tester or a toothpick inserted in the center comes out clean. Cool the layers in the pans on a wire rack for 5 minutes; then remove them from the pans by inverting them onto the wire rack, and continue to cool them.

5. Place one cake layer on a plate, and spread frosting evenly over the top. Set the second layer on top of the first, and spread the frosting on the sides of the cake layers and over the top.

Serves 10 to 12.

CREAM CHEESE FROSTING

1. Beat the butter and cream cheese together in the large bowl of an electric mixer. Add the sugar, vanilla, and 2 tablespoons of the milk, and mix until of good spreading consistency. Add more milk if necessary.

Yields frosting for 1 double-layer cake.

NANA JO'S CHOCOLATE PIE

In 1920, shortly after her marriage to Clarence Fitzpatrick, Jack Fitzpatrick's mother, Clara Jones, took a course at Fanny Farmer's Cooking School in Boston, where she acquired this recipe for Chocolate Pie. Although not currently offered at The Red Lion Inn, it nevertheless remains a family favorite.

2 cups milk

2 ounces unsweetened chocolate

1 cup sugar

1/2 cup flour

1/2 teaspoon salt

2 eggs, separated

2 teaspoons vanilla

1 baked pie shell (*recipe follows*)

lightly sweetened whipped cream

1. In a double boiler, over simmering water, heat 1 1/2 cups of the milk with the chocolate. Mix well until the chocolate is melted (it will remain suspended in tiny droplets in the milk).

2. Combine the sugar, flour, and salt in a small bowl. Add the remaining 1/2 cup milk, and stir to create a paste. Add this to the chocolate mixture in the pan, and heat over medium heat, stirring until thick, about 10 minutes. Reduce the heat to low, cover, and cook for 15 minutes, stirring occasionally.

3. Whisk the egg yolks slightly in a small bowl, and mix in a spoonful or two of the chocolate mixture. When it is smooth, add the yolks to the chocolate mixture. Cook for 2 minutes, stirring constantly.

4. Beat the egg whites to form soft peaks. Carefully fold them into the chocolate mixture until they are completely blended. Allow them to cool, then add the vanilla. (The filling may be held for 24 hours at this point.)

5. Pour the filling into the baked pie shell. Chill and serve with whipped cream.

Yields 1 pie.

¹/₄ **cup butter, cold**

¹/₄ **cup shortening**

1 cup + 2 tablespoons flour

¹/₂ **teaspoon salt**

¹/₄ **cup milk, cold**

PIE CRUST FOR ONE-CRUST PIE

1. Blend the butter and shortening together with a wooden spoon in a small bowl.

2. Sift the flour and salt together into a large bowl. Cut in the butter and shortening, using a pastry blender or two knives, until the mixture resembles cornmeal. Add the cold milk, and blend until it is absorbed. Roll the dough into a ball. Wrap it in plastic wrap, and refrigerate until chilled, about 30 minutes. (Or, if using a food processor, place the butter, shortening, flour, and salt in the bowl; fit with a steel blade. Process until the mixture reaches the consistency of cornmeal. With the processor on, add the milk slowly through the funnel until the dough forms a ball.)

3. When you are ready to bake the pie shell, preheat the oven to 400°. To bake a one-crust pie shell, fit the crust into the pie plate, and flute the edge. Prick the bottom and sides of the crust with a fork.

4. If the shell will be filled with a cream filling that will not be baked further, place a piece of parchment paper the size of the pie plate inside the pie shell, then scatter pie weights or beans on the bottom to weight it. This helps the shell to retain its shape. The shell should be baked at 400° for 8 to 10 minutes, or until the fluted edge is a golden brown. The weights and parchment should be removed after 5 minutes of baking.

5. If the shell will receive a filling that requires further baking, the crust should be prebaked 5 minutes only, without the addition of the parchment paper and weights.

Yields 1 crust.

PECAN PIE

1. Preheat the oven to 325°.

2. In a large bowl, mix all the filling ingredients together, except the pecan halves. Stir thoroughly.

3. Arrange the pecan halves in a single layer in the bottom of the unbaked pie shell, and pour the filling into the shell.

4. Bake at 325° for 1 hour, or until set. Cool well before serving.

Yields 1 pie.

$^2/_3$ cup dark corn syrup

$^2/_3$ cup light corn syrup

4 eggs, lightly beaten

$^3/_4$ cup sugar

$^1/_3$ cup butter, melted

1 teaspoon vanilla

$^1/_8$ teaspoon salt

1 $^1/_3$ cups chopped pecans

1 cup pecan halves

1 unbaked pie shell (*see page 132*)

ART MARASCO

A Wooton desk, one of the many antiques throughout The Red Lion Inn.

$^1/_2$ cup + 1 tablespoon butter, melted

1 cup light brown sugar, firmly packed

2 eggs

$^1/_2$ teaspoon vanilla

1 $^1/_3$ cups flour

1 $^1/_4$ teaspoons baking powder

$^1/_4$ teaspoon salt

1 package semisweet chocolate chips (6 ounces)

$^1/_2$ cup walnuts, chopped

Hot Fudge Sauce (*recipe below*)

$^1/_3$ cup water

1 tablespoon butter

2 ounces unsweetened chocolate, coarsely chopped

1 cup granulated sugar

2 tablespoons light corn syrup

pinch of salt

1 teaspoon vanilla

CHOCOLATE CHIP PIE

This pie is one of the specialties of The Red Lion Inn. It's a sweet-tooth's dream, especially when served warm, and topped with vanilla ice cream and hot fudge sauce, as it was featured in *Chocolatier* magazine in 1986.

1. Preheat the oven to 325°. Lightly butter a 9" pie plate.

2. Beat $^1/_2$ cup of the melted butter and the sugar together in a large bowl. Add the eggs and vanilla, and mix thoroughly.

3. Sift the flour, baking powder, and salt together. Add to the creamed mixture and mix together.

4. Stir in the chocolate chips and nuts. (The dough will resemble chocolate chip cookie dough.)

5. Place the dough in the prepared pie plate. Flatten and smooth it out with a broad wooden spoon or your hand. Bake at 325° for 30 to 40 minutes, or until a toothpick inserted in the center comes out clean. Brush the pie with the remaining 1 tablespoon melted butter as soon as it comes from the oven. Cool and serve with ice cream and hot fudge sauce.

Yields 1 pie.

HOT FUDGE SAUCE

1. In a heavy saucepan, over medium heat, bring the water and butter to a simmer and heat until the butter is melted. Remove the pan from the heat and stir in the chocolate. Continue stirring until it has melted.

2. Add the sugar, corn syrup, and salt, and mix well. Return the pan to the heat and bring the mixture to a boil without stirring. Cover and cook for 3 minutes, then uncover and simmer for 2 minutes longer. Remove from the heat and cool for 5 minutes. Stir in the vanilla and serve.

Yields 1 cup.

PUMPKIN PIE

1. Preheat the oven to 325°.

2. In a large bowl, stir all the ingredients together well, and pour into the prepared pie shells.

3. Bake at 325° for 45 to 60 minutes, until set (a thin knife inserted in the center should come out clean).

Yields 2 pies.

9 eggs

6 cups canned pumpkin

3 cups evaporated milk

3 cups whole milk

3 cups light brown sugar, firmly packed

1 tablespoon ground cinnamon

1 1/2 teaspoons ground ginger

3/4 teaspoon ground cloves

3/4 teaspoon ground nutmeg

3/4 teaspoon salt

2 unbaked pie shells

3 cups cake flour, sifted

2 cups sugar

1 cup unsweetened cocoa

$1/2$ teaspoon salt

2 teaspoons baking soda

1 cup sour cream

1 $1/4$ cups vegetable oil

1 cup hot water

2 eggs

1 tablespoon vanilla

Dark Chocolate Buttercream Icing
(*recipe below*)

CHOCOLATE DEVIL'S FOOD CAKE

1. Preheat the oven to 350°. Grease and flour two 10" round cake pans.

2. Sift all dry ingredients together. Set aside.

3. Mix the sour cream, oil, hot water, eggs, and vanilla together in a large bowl. Beat in the dry ingredients and mix thoroughly.

4. Pour the batter into the prepared cake pans. Bake at 350° for 30 to 35 minutes, or until a toothpick inserted in the center comes out clean. Cool the layers in the pans on a wire rack for 5 minutes; then remove them from the pans by inverting them onto the wire rack, and continue to cool them.

5. Place one cake layer on a plate, and spread the icing evenly over the top. Set the second layer on top of the first, and spread icing on the sides of the cake layers and over the top.

Yields 1 double-layer cake.

1 $1/2$ cups butter, softened

1 cup + 2 tablespoons unsweetened cocoa

4 cups confectioners' sugar

$1/2$ cup + 2 tablespoons milk

1 $1/2$ teaspoons vanilla

DARK CHOCOLATE BUTTERCREAM ICING

1. Cream the butter well in a large bowl. Cream in the remaining ingredients, beating well. If the icing is too thick to spread, you may add more milk.

Yields icing for 1 double-layer cake.

CHEESECAKE WITH NEW ENGLAND BLUEBERRY SAUCE

1. Preheat the oven to 350°.

2. **Prepare the crust:** Combine the graham cracker crumbs and sugar in a bowl. Pour in the melted butter and mix until all the crumbs are moistened.

3. Press the mixture into a 10" springform pan, thoroughly covering the bottom and pressing it to the top of the sides. Bake at 350° for 10 minutes. Set the crust aside to cool at least 10 minutes.

4. **For the filling:** Cream the cream cheese and sugar together in the large bowl of an electric mixer. Mix in the remaining ingredients, and beat at medium speed for about 2 1/2 minutes, scraping the bowl once. Pour into the cooled crust.

5. Bake at 350° for 40 minutes, rotating the pan *gently* once during the baking. Turn off the oven heat, and leave the cheesecake in the oven for an additional 30 to 45 minutes until set, rotating the pan twice. Then remove the cheesecake from the oven and allow it to cool thoroughly. Cover and chill overnight or for at least 3 hours.

6. Pour the topping on the top of the cheesecake before serving, spreading it so it covers the center.

Serves 10 to 12.

For the crust:

1 1/2 cups graham cracker crumbs

1/4 cup sugar

1/3 cup butter, melted

For the filling:

24 ounces cream cheese (3 large packages), softened

1 1/2 cups sugar

6 eggs, at room temperature

2 cups sour cream, at room temperature

2 tablespoons cornstarch

1 tablespoon lemon juice

2 teaspoons vanilla

New England Blueberry Sauce (*recipe follows*)

3 cups blueberries

¹/₄ cup sugar

2 tablespoons lemon juice

2 ¹/₂ teaspoons cornstarch

New England Blueberry Sauce

1. Combine 2 cups of the blueberries, the sugar, and 1 tablespoon of the lemon juice in a saucepan, and cook over high heat until boiling.

2. Mix the remaining 1 tablespoon of lemon juice with the cornstarch, and add to the blueberries. Cook, stirring constantly, over medium heat, until thickened. Remove from the heat, and stir in the remaining 1 cup blueberries. Cover and chill until ready to serve.

Yields 2 cups.

2 ¹/₂ pounds apples, peeled, cored, and sliced

2 cups blackberries, fresh or frozen

1 cup sugar

1 ¹/₂ teaspoons ground cinnamon

¹/₂ teaspoon ground nutmeg

2 tablespoons flour

1 tablespoon butter

pie crust for a two-crust pie (*see page 129*)

1 egg yolk

1 tablespoon milk

Blackberry and Apple Pie

1. Preheat the oven to 375°.

2. Mix the apples and blackberries together in a large bowl.

3. Blend the dry ingredients together, and then gently mix into the fruit. Spoon the filling into the prepared pie crust, and dot with butter. Top with the remaining pie crust. Crimp the edges of the top and bottom crusts together, sealing the fruit into the shell. Whisk the egg yolk and milk together, and brush this wash over the top crust. Pierce the top pie crust several times with a knife, to allow steam to escape.

4. Bake at 375° for 1 ¹/₄ hours, until the apples are tender when poked with a thin knife. (If crust seems to be browning too quickly, reduce the heat to 325°.)

Yields 1 pie.

TRIPLE CHOCOLATE CHEESECAKE

1. Preheat the oven to 325°. Lightly grease a 10" springform pan.

2. Place the cookie crumbs in a medium bowl and mix them thoroughly with the melted butter until the crumbs are coated. Press the cookie mixture over the bottom and 1" up the sides of the prepared pan. Bake at 325° for 5 to 10 minutes. Remove from oven and allow to cool.

3. Melt 6 ounces of the chocolate in the top of a double boiler over simmering water. Cool.

4. Cream the cream cheese well in the large bowl of an electric mixer. Add the melted chocolate and mix thoroughly. Add the eggs, one at a time, mixing well after each, then stir in the sugar, flour, and vanilla.

5. Pour the batter into the prepared crust. Bake at 325° for about 40 minutes, or until the edge is set and the center is still darker and rather "shaky." Cool completely. Remove from the pan and place on a pretty plate.

6. Combine the remaining 8 ounces chocolate and the cream in a small saucepan and cook over low heat, stirring frequently, until the chocolate has melted. Spread the glaze over the top of the cheesecake, and let it drip down the sides.

7. Thinly slice each strawberry down to the stem, creating a fan shape. Garnish each slice of cheesecake with a strawberry "fan."

Yields 16 servings.

1 $^1/_2$ cups chocolate cookie wafers, finely ground

$^1/_4$ cups butter, melted

14 ounces semi-sweet chocolate

2 pounds cream cheese, at room temperature

5 large eggs

$^3/_4$ cup sugar

3 tablespoons flour

1 $^1/_2$ teaspoons vanilla

7 tablespoons heavy cream

16 strawberries

APPLE HILL DESIGN

A contented lion.

PUDDINGS, PASTRIES, AND DESSERTS

There are grunts, duffs, flummeries, pandowdies, slumps, cobblers, fools, buckles, syllabubs, and tansies — all quaint, old-fashioned names that often confound us today. Were our foremothers playing word tricks, knowing future generations would never break the secret code?

Even leading food writers disagree on exact directions for making these revered desserts. A grunt, for example, according to *The American Heritage Cookbook,* is made by cooking the fruit, pouring it in a baking dish, dropping biscuit dough on top, covering it tightly, and placing it in a pan of hot water in a heated oven where it will steam for 1 ½ hours. Betty Crocker agrees, but James Beard says a grunt is baked, and not steamed, and Time-Life's *American Cooking: New England* insists it's made just like a slump, in which the fruit is cooked on top of the stove, with biscuit dough dropped in, and then covered, and cooked stove-top, for 30 minutes. (Louisa May Alcott, author of *Little Women,* loved slump so much that she named her house in Concord, Massachusetts, "Apple Slump.")

There's just as much controversy over flummeries. In her *New England Cookbook,* Eleanor Early says to line a loaf pan with slices of bread, and then to alternate cooked berries with buttered slices of bread, ending with a piece of bread, and then to bake it. However, *The American Heritage Cookbook* describes a concoction similar to a custard, attributing it to the Shakers (who had many settlements near Stockbridge). This cookbook claims the Shakers developed flummeries for the aged in their community, who had difficulty chewing. This version is a molded dish of berries, milk, cornstarch, and sugar, generally served with whipped cream or sweetened berries.

Similarly, cobblers are confused with pandowdies, but the dish known as fool is universally described as fruit cooked on the stove until very tender and then pureed and cooled before it is folded into whipped cream. For an exercise in the absolutely ridiculous, however, few recipes can top Amelia Simmons' for syllabub in *American Cookery,* in which she recommends milking the cow directly into the dessert to froth it.

The Red Lion Inn's Blackberry Tansey is much more sensible. It's a scrumptious concoction that starts with berries cooked on the stove, and ends as a baked dish topped with breadcrumbs — and it's as pretty as it is good.

Desserts at The Red Lion Inn follow the homey, comfortable tradition of desserts in the homes of early settlers. Apple crisp, bread pudding, Indian pudding, and tapioca are still served in Red Lion Inn dining rooms much as they were in colonial homes and taverns.

The Red Lion Inn sign.

6 cups milk

¹/₂ cup butter

¹/₂ cup + 2 tablespoons cornmeal

2 eggs

2 ²/₃ cups molasses

3 tablespoons ground cinnamon

1 tablespoon ground ginger

1 cup apples, peeled, cored, and
    thinly sliced

¹/₂ cup raisins

"Aunt Mert" Plumb, co-owner with her husband Charles, and later their nephews, from 1862 to 1952, used a handwritten cookbook in the Red Lion Inn's kitchen. Her recipe for the thrifty New England favorite that she called "Mother's Indian Pudding" probably originated some time prior to 1879 and reads "3 cups molasses, 5 cups flour, 1 cup sour milk, 2T ginger, ²/₃ cup butter and 2 eggs."

INDIAN PUDDING

Indian pudding is the oldest of New England desserts, and many people think it is the best. Early New Englanders baked it on Saturday, in the same oven as the baked beans. The pudding cooked for ten hours in the oven, and was eaten for supper, dished up in a soup plate and drowned in thick, sweet cream. Here is the very old, very New England, very Red Lion Inn version, which fortunately takes only two hours to cook. Indian pudding is best if made a day before it is eaten.

1. Preheat the oven to 300°. Butter a 2 ¹/₂ to 3-quart shallow ovenproof dish.

2. Combine 5 cups of the milk with the butter, in a saucepan, and bring just to the boiling point.

3. Combine the remaining 1 cup milk with the cornmeal, and add to the scalded milk. Cook for 20 minutes over low heat, stirring slowly so the mixture does not burn.

4. Mix the eggs, molasses, and spices together. Add to the thickened cornmeal mixture, whisking thoroughly. Pour the mixture into the prepared casserole dish, and bake in a 300° oven for 1 hour.

5. Stir the apples and raisins into the pudding. Bake at 300° for 1 hour more, or until a toothpick inserted in the center comes out clean.

6. Serve warm, topped with ice cream and/or whipped cream.

Serves 10 to 12.

RICE PUDDING

1. Combine the rice, water, and salt in the top of a double boiler, and place the pan directly on the heat. Bring to a boil, cover, and simmer until the water is almost absorbed, 35 to 40 minutes.

2. Add the condensed milk and egg to the rice, stirring well. Place the pan over simmering water, and cook, continuing to stir, until thickened but still creamy, about 10 minutes. Cool slightly.

3. Stir the vanilla and raisins into the rice. Serve warm; or serve chilled, topped with whipped cream and a dash of nutmeg.

Serves 8.

1/2 cup white rice

2 1/2 cups water

1/8 teaspoon salt

1 can (16 ounces) sweetened condensed milk

1 egg, beaten

1 teaspoon vanilla

2 tablespoons raisins

whipped cream (if served cold)

dash ground nutmeg (if served cold)

CRÈME CARAMEL

1. Preheat the oven to 300°.

2. Combine the sugar and water in a heavy saucepan, and cook over high heat, stirring constantly, until golden and caramelized, about 5 minutes. Pour the caramel into six custard cups, gently swirling to coat the bottoms. Allow the caramel to harden in the cups.

3. In a bowl, whisk the egg yolk, whole eggs, vanilla, and nutmeg together. Add the milk, sugar, and salt, and whisk well.

4. Evenly fill the custard cups with the egg mixture. Set the custard cups in a pan filled with water that comes halfway up the sides of the cups. Place the pan in the oven, and bake at 300° for 20 minutes. Revolve the pan 180 degrees and bake an additional 35 to 45 minutes, or until a knife inserted down the side of the custard comes out clean.

Serves 6.

3/4 cup sugar

2 1/2 tablespoons water

1 egg yolk

3 whole eggs

1 teaspoon vanilla

1/4 teaspoon ground nutmeg

3 cups milk

1/2 cup plus 2 tablespoons sugar

1/8 teaspoon salt

1 loaf white bread (1 pound), crusts removed and bread cubed

4 cups milk

7 eggs

1 teaspoon vanilla

1 ¼ cups sugar

¼ cup raisins

Red Lion Inn Bread Pudding

1. Preheat the oven to 300°. Butter an 8" x 8" ovenproof pan.

2. Place the bread cubes in the prepared baking pan.

3. Mix the milk, eggs, vanilla, and sugar together, and pour over the bread. Press down on the bread with a spoon to make sure it is thoroughly saturated with the liquid. Bake at 300° for 20 minutes.

4. Stir the pudding and sprinkle the raisins over the top. Press the pudding down to cover the raisins with liquid. Bake for another 1 ½ hours. The pudding is done when a knife inserted in the center (all the way to the bottom of the pan) comes out clean.

Serves 8.

Apple Crisp

Jane Fitzpatrick contributed this cherished family recipe to the inn. If apples are not available, peaches are an excellent substitute.

4 cups tart apples (Cortlands are excellent), cored, peeled, and sliced (about 6 to 8 apples)

½ cup water

¾ cup flour

½ cup white sugar

½ cup light brown sugar, firmly packed

1 teaspoon ground cinnamon

½ teaspoon salt

½ cup butter, softened

1. Preheat the oven to 350°. Butter a deep ovenproof baking dish.

2. Arrange the apple slices in the prepared baking dish, and pour the water over them.

3. In a mixing bowl, stir together the flour, sugars, cinnamon, and salt. Cut in the butter with a pastry blender, fork, or your fingers, until the mixture resembles tiny pebbles. Spread the topping over the apples. Bake at 350° until the apples are tender and the crust is brown, about 35 to 45 minutes.

4. Serve warm, topped with ice cream or whipped cream.

Serves 6.

BAKED APPLES RED LION

1. Preheat the oven to 425°. Butter an ovenproof casserole with sides at least 1" high, large enough to hold 6 apples.

2. Combine the water and bourbon in a small bowl, and soak all the raisins in the liquid for 2 to 3 hours, until plump. Stuff the raisins into the apples.

3. Melt the butter in a saucepan, stir in the flour, and cook gently for 2 minutes. Remove from the heat, and stir in the brown sugar and vanilla. Spread the sugar mixture over the top of the apples. Place the apples in the prepared casserole, and bake at 425° until a crust is set on top, about 20 minutes. Lower the oven temperature to 350° and bake until the apples are tender, about 30 minutes more.

4. Serve with brandy-flavored whipped cream, or with ice cream.

Serves 6.

1/2 cup water

3 tablespoons bourbon

1/2 cup dark raisins

1/2 cup golden raisins

6 tart apples, cored and peeled halfway down

3 tablespoons butter, melted

2 tablespoons flour

1/2 cup light brown sugar, firmly packed

1/2 teaspoon vanilla

vanilla ice cream or brandy-flavored whipped cream, for topping

GRAPENUT PUDDING

1. Preheat the oven to 350°. Butter an 8" square ovenproof pan.

2. Place the milk in a saucepan, and bring it just to a boil.

3. Mix the grapenuts, sugar, and salt together in a bowl. Add them to the scalded milk and cook for 2 to 3 minutes, over medium heat. Remove from the heat and stir one-fourth of the hot milk into the beaten eggs and mix thoroughly. Pour the eggs back into the pan, and return the mixture to the heat, stirring continuously until thickened, about 10 minutes.

4. Pour the pudding into the prepared pan, and bake at 350° for 30 minutes. Stir, and serve warm, topped with ice cream, whipped cream, or yogurt.

Serves 6.

4 cups milk

2/3 cup grapenut cereal (not flakes)

2/3 cup sugar

dash salt

2 eggs, beaten

vanilla ice cream, whipped cream, or yogurt, for topping

1 cup rolled oats

1 cup flour

1 cup light brown sugar, firmly packed

$1/4$ teaspoon baking soda

$1/4$ teaspoon baking powder

$1/4$ teaspoon salt

$1/2$ cup butter, melted

3 $1/2$ pounds (about 7 large) tart apples

$1/2$ cup cranberries

$3/4$ cup sugar

1 $1/2$ teaspoons ground cinnamon

APPLE-CRANBERRY CRISP

1. Preheat the oven to 450°. Butter the bottom of an 8" x 8" baking pan.

2. In a large bowl, mix together the rolled oats, flour, brown sugar, baking soda, baking powder, and salt. Add the melted butter and blend well, until all the dry ingredients are moistened.

3. Peel, core, and slice the apples. Place them in another large bowl, and mix with the cranberries. Add the sugar and cinnamon, and toss well.

4. Place $1/3$ of the oat mixture in the prepared baking pan, pressing it down. Pour in the apple/cranberry mixture. Cover with the remaining oat mixture. Cover the pan with aluminum foil, and bake at 450° for 1 $1/4$ hours, or until the apples are tender, removing the foil during the last quarter hour of cooking to brown the top.

Serves 8 to 10.

BLACKBERRY TANSEY

This dish is equally good with blueberries, although you should substitute 1 tablespoon lemon juice for 1 tablespoon of the blackberry juice.

2 cups blackberries

1 tablespoon water

$1/4$ teaspoon ground nutmeg

1 tablespoon cornstarch

2 eggs

$1/2$ cup sugar

2 tablespoons butter, melted

2 cups dried bread crumbs

vanilla ice cream or whipped cream, for topping

1. Preheat the oven to 350°. Butter an 8" x 8" baking dish, or a 10" pie pan.

2. Rinse the blackberries in cold water, removing any impurities. Combine the blackberries and water in a saucepan, and cook gently over low heat about 6 minutes, until light purple and juicy.

3. Remove $1/2$ cup of the berry juice, and combine it with the nutmeg and cornstarch in another small saucepan. Cook over medium heat until thickened, about 5 minutes. Add the cooked berries and any remaining juice, and stir together.

4. In a mixing bowl, beat the eggs, sugar, and butter together until blended. Add the bread crumbs and toss to moisten them.

5. Pour the blackberry mixture into the prepared baking pan, and spoon the breadcrumb mixture over the top. Bake at 350° for 20 to 30 minutes, or until lightly browned on top.

6. Serve warm, with whipped cream or ice cream.

Serves 6.

1 egg

2 tablespoons tapioca, quick
  cooking

$^1/_4$ cup sugar

$^1/_8$ teaspoon salt

2 cups milk

$^1/_2$ teaspoon vanilla

$^1/_2$ teaspoon ground cinnamon

$^1/_8$ teaspoon ground nutmeg

> "Tapioca puddings, like cornstarch
> puddings, were a children's dessert in New
> England. So when the children grew up,
> they wouldn't eat them any more. When
> girls got to college, they called tapioca
> 'freshman's tears' and cornstarch 'baby's
> flannel petticoat.'"
>
> New England Cookbook

1 bunch green seedless grapes
  (about 40 to 50 grapes)

$^1/_2$ cup honey

2 tablespoons lime juice

2 tablespoons fresh mint, finely
  chopped

$^1/_2$ cup plain yogurt

SPICED TAPIOCA

1. Beat the egg and place it in the top of a double boiler over simmering water. Immediately add the tapioca, sugar, salt and milk and stir well. Cook, stirring frequently until it thickens moderately, about 12 to 15 minutes. Remove the pan from the heat. Add the vanilla, cinnamon, and nutmeg.

2. Pour the pudding into a shallow container to cool, covering the surface with plastic wrap to prevent a skin from forming. The pudding will thicken to the consistency of mayonnaise as it cools.

Serves 4.

HONEY-MINTED GRAPES WITH YOGURT

1. Wash and stem the grapes. Place them in a bowl.

2. Combine the honey, lime juice, and 1 $^1/_2$ tablespoons of the mint. Pour this over the grapes, mix well, and refrigerate for several hours or overnight.

3. Divide the grapes among 4 stemmed dessert or sherbet glasses. Top each serving with 2 tablespoons of yogurt. Sprinkle the remaining chopped mint on top as a garnish (or garnish with a thin round of fresh lime).

Serves 4.

COOKIES AND CANDIES

Ann Brown is Jack and Jane Fitzpatrick's youngest daughter. From childhood, she has been creative and inventive — and she loves fantasy. So in 1975, several years out of college, she formed her own company, creating whimsical fantasies from gumdrops, necco wafers, a white icing, and other candies. She called the company Gum Drop Square, selling her confections to Bloomingdale's, Neiman-Marcus, Filene's, and others. For Bloomingdale's she designed a four-foot-tall Santa Claus that she constructed in their window. It attracted the attention of Imelda Marcos, who bought it for $450 and slipped it away to her suite at the Waldorf-Astoria. For Neiman-Marcus, Ann designed a 500-pound replica of Bunratty Castle.

But Ann's most stupendous creation was for Macy's in New York. For them, she designed a candy castle made of over 1 million pieces of candy and weighing over a ton. She had to ship it to New York in eight pieces.

She also designed a candy model of the U.S. "Eagle" as a centerpiece for a dinner commemorating the end of the "Tall Ships" transatlantic race for the U.S. bicentennial in 1976, a model of the Boston City Hall, a replica of St. Basil's Cathedral in Moscow, and a seven-foot candy statue of George Washington that weighed 282 pounds.

The inn is fortunate to have several of Ann's candy sculptures itself. Notable among them is a candy replica of Main Street in Stockbridge, a candy castle, a 3 1/2 foot tall gumdrop Santa Claus, and a 12-foot candy train. All come out at Christmas, wisely accompanied by glass bowls of gumdrops to divert curious fingers that might otherwise pluck one from Santa's big tummy.

The Red Lion Inn also specializes in cookie and candy edibles. The brownies and chocolate chip cookies are legendary, as are the chocolate covered strawberries. Truffles and bourbon balls are easy confections to make at home, and strawberry delights are attractive garnishments for other desserts.

Replica of Main Street, Stockbridge, in candy and gumdrops — part of the Red Lion Christmas decorations.

CLEMENS KALISCHER

4 ounces unsweetened chocolate

$^1/_2$ cup butter

4 eggs

2 cups sugar

$^1/_4$ teaspoon salt

1 tablespoon vanilla

1 cup flour

$^3/_4$ cup walnuts, chopped

vanilla ice cream (optional)

Hot Fudge Sauce (optional, *see page 134*)

RED LION INN BROWNIES

These fudgy brownies are among the most popular requests at The Red Lion Inn. They're often served on large silver trays as dessert for business luncheons, or beside the coffee table at evening cocktail parties. They are regularly offered on the menu, topped with vanilla ice cream and hot fudge sauce, for a chocolate lover's dream come true.

1. Preheat the oven to 325°. Line an 8" square baking pan with lightly buttered parchment paper.

2. Melt the chocolate and butter in a double boiler over simmering water, stirring frequently. Remove from the heat, and set aside to cool.

3. In a mixing bowl, beat the eggs together until frothy. Add the sugar, and blend it in well; then gently fold in the melted chocolate mixture, salt, and vanilla. Stir in the flour and walnuts, and stir just until blended.

4. Spread the batter in the prepared pan. Bake until it is crusty on top and almost firm to the touch, about 30 to 35 minutes. *Do not overbake.* Cool completely in the pan and then cut into squares. Serve, if you desire, with a scoop of ice cream on top, covered by Hot Fudge Sauce.

Yields 24 brownies.

> *"...There is one country inn to which I feel very close. That's the Red Lion Inn in Stockbridge.... Like all of the residents of my village, I have a proprietary interest in the inn...."*
>
> *Norman Simpson,* The Berkshire Traveller

HOLIDAY APPLE SQUARES

This is a traditional holiday recipe from Chef Mongeon's family, brought by his grandmother from her home in Quebec many years ago. Although not generally served at The Red Lion Inn, they are a regular treat in the Mongeon household.

1 cup butter, softened

2 cups sugar

4 jumbo eggs

1 teaspoon almond extract

3 cups flour, sifted

Apple Filling (*recipe below*)

2 tablespoons confectioners' sugar

1 tablespoon water

1. Preheat the oven to 350°. Butter the bottom and sides of a 10" x 15" x 1" rimmed cookie sheet.

2. Cream the butter in a mixing bowl. Add the sugar and cream it in well.

3. Beat the eggs in a small bowl, and add them to the sugar mixture; blend well. Add the almond extract and flour, and mix thoroughly. Spread three-fourths of the mixture over the prepared cookie sheet.

4. Spread the fruit filling over the pastry mixture; then spread the rest of the batter over the fruit. Bake at 350° for 45 minutes. Allow the squares to cool slightly.

5. Mix the confectioners' sugar with the water to form a glaze. Brush the glaze over the warm pastry. When the pastry has cooled completely, cut it into squares.

Yields 16 squares.

APPLE FILLING

$^1/_2$ cup loosely packed light brown sugar

1 tablespoon ground cinnamon

dash ground cloves

1 teaspoon ground nutmeg

$^1/_2$ cup raisins

8 McIntosh apples, peeled, cored, and sliced

1 cup apple cider

1. Place all the ingredients in a large saucepan, and stir well. Cover and cook over medium heat, stirring frequently, until the apples begin to cook down, about 12 minutes. Cool thoroughly — at least 30 minutes.

Yields filling for 16 squares.

^{1}/$_4$ **cup butter, softened**

1 cup light brown sugar, firmly
packed

1 egg

^{1}/$_2$ **cup walnuts, chopped**

1 teaspoon vanilla

^{2}/$_3$ **cup flour**

1 teaspoon baking powder

^{1}/$_8$ **teaspoon salt**

NANA PRATT'S
BROWN SUGAR SQUARES

Nana Pratt was the mother of Jane Fitzpatrick, Red Lion Inn owner. Although these are not regularly served at the inn, you may find them added for special occasions.

1. Preheat the oven to 350°. Butter an 8" square pan.

2. Cream the butter in a mixing bowl. Add the brown sugar, egg, walnuts, and vanilla, and beat well.

3. Sift the flour, baking powder, and salt together. Add them to the butter mixture, and beat thoroughly.

4. Spread the dough in the prepared pan, and bake at 350° for 30 minutes, being careful not to overbake. The cookies are done when a toothpick is inserted in the center comes out clean. Allow them to cool in the pan, then cut into squares.

Yields 9 to 12 squares.

HERMITS

This recipe came to The Red Lion Inn from Marcia Kneissel, the inn's baker — it's one she learned from her mother. These will be prepared at the inn for special occasions.

1. Preheat the oven to 350°. Butter a 9" x 13" ovenproof baking pan.

2. Sift the flour, sugar, salt, baking soda, cloves, ginger, and cinnamon together into a large mixing bowl.

3. In a separate bowl, mix the oil, egg, molasses, and water. Add this to dry ingredients, and mix well. Stir in the raisins. The dough will be thick and may be easiest to mix with your hands.

4. Spread the dough in the prepared pan, and bake at 350° for 20 minutes. Cool in the pan, then cut into squares.

Yields 12 squares.

3 cups flour

1 ¹/₄ cups sugar

¹/₂ teaspoon salt

1 ¹/₂ teaspoons baking soda

1 teaspoon ground cloves

1 teaspoon ground ginger

1 teaspoon ground cinnamon

¹/₂ cup vegetable oil

1 egg

¹/₄ cup molasses

5 tablespoons water

¹/₂ cup raisins

"New England cooks had a penchant for giving odd names to their dishes — apparently for no other reason than the fun of saying them. Cookies were no exception. Snickerdoodles come from a tradition of this sort that includes Graham Jakes, Jolly Boys, Brambles, Tangle Breeches and Kinkawoodles."

The American Heritage Cookbook

$^1/_2$ cup butter, softened

$^3/_4$ cup sugar

2 egg yolks

$^3/_4$ teaspoon vanilla

1 tablespoon milk

1 $^1/_2$ cups flour

$^1/_4$ teaspoon salt

$^1/_4$ teaspoon baking powder

Sugar Cookie Frosting (*recipe below*)

DECORATED SUGAR COOKIES

These frosted, cut-out sugar cookies are ideal for a child's first attempts at baking. Christmas trees painted with bright green frosting, red hearts for Valentine's Day, and orange pumpkins for Halloween are fun to make and delight both youngsters and adults.

1. Cream the butter until very fluffy in a medium-sized bowl. Add the sugar, and blend it in well. Beat in the egg yolks, vanilla, and milk.

2. Sift the flour with the salt and baking powder, and add to the creamed mixture, mixing well. Form the dough into a ball, wrap in plastic wrap, and refrigerate until firm, at least 1 hour.

3. Preheat the oven to 350°. Line a large baking sheet with lightly buttered parchment paper.

4. Roll the dough out to $^1/_4$" thickness on a floured board. Flour your choice of cookie cutters, and cut out the cookies. Place them on the prepared cookie sheet. Bake at 350° for 8 to 10 minutes, until golden. Remove the cookies from the sheet and place them on a rack to cool. Paint the cooled cookies with the prepared frosting.

Yields 42 to 60 cookies.

4 $^1/_2$ cups confectioners' sugar, sifted

$^1/_4$ cup milk

$^1/_2$ teaspoon vanilla

food coloring (optional)

SUGAR COOKIE FROSTING

1. Mix the confectioners' sugar, milk, and vanilla together. If the frosting is too thick to spread, add more milk. Add various colors of food coloring to small amounts of the frosting, for decorating as desired.

OATMEAL BUTTERSCOTCH COOKIES

This recipe is sometimes varied at The Red Lion Inn by using currants in place of the butterscotch bits.

1. Preheat the oven to 350°. Line a baking sheet with lightly oiled parchment paper.

2. Cream the butter and brown sugar together in a bowl, until fluffy.

3. Add the eggs and water, and blend them in well. Beat in the flour, baking powder, baking soda, and salt. Finally, stir in the oats and butterscotch bits.

4. Drop 1 1/2" balls of the dough onto the prepared cookie sheet. Bake at 350° for 8 to 12 minutes, until golden. Allow the cookies to cool slightly (about 3 minutes) on the baking sheet, then transfer them to a wire rack to cool.

Yields 3 to 4 dozen cookies.

1 cup butter, softened

1 1/2 cups light brown sugar, firmly packed

2 eggs

4 teaspoons water

2 cups flour

2 teaspoons baking powder

1 teaspoon baking soda

1 teaspoon salt

1 1/2 cups rolled oats

2 cups butterscotch bits

1 cup butter, softened

$^3/_4$ cup light brown sugar, firmly
    packed

$^3/_4$ cup white sugar

2 eggs

1 teaspoon vanilla

2 $^1/_4$ cups flour

1 teaspoon baking soda

$^1/_2$ teaspoon salt

1 large (12 ounce) package
    chocolate chips

RED LION INN
CHOCOLATE CHIP COOKIES

Along with Red Lion Inn Brownies, these Chocolate Chip Cookies top
the list of requested favorites.

1. Preheat the oven to 350°. Line a baking sheet with lightly buttered
   parchment paper.

2. Cream the butter in a mixing bowl. Add the sugars, and blend them in well.
   Then add the eggs and vanilla, creaming thoroughly.

3. Mix the flour with the baking soda and salt. Stir into the sugar mixture.
   Finally, gently stir in chocolate chips.

4. Drop the dough in 1 $^1/_2$" balls, onto the prepared baking sheet. Bake at 350°
   for 8 to 12 minutes, or until golden on top. Allow the cookies to cool
   slightly (about 3 minutes) on the baking sheet, then transfer them to a wire
   rack to cool.

Yields 3 $^1/_2$ dozen cookies.

"Of all of the places I've been
    to wine in, to dine in
    to have a good time in
    you can't beat an Old Country Inn"

Poem in the Red Lion Inn's scrapbook,
penned by an anonymous guest

WHOOPIE PIES

1. Preheat the oven to 350°. Line a baking sheet with parchment paper.

2. Cream the shortening, sugar, egg, milk, and vanilla together thoroughly in a bowl.

3. Mix the flour, baking soda, salt, cocoa, and oil together in another bowl. Add to the creamed mixture and blend.

4. Drop the batter by spoonfuls onto the prepared baking sheet, spacing them 2" apart. Bake in 350° oven for 8 to 10 minutes, until done. Allow to cool slightly on the baking sheet, and then transfer them to a wire rack to cool.

5. To assemble a "pie," spread some filling on one chocolate cookie, and top with a second cookie. Repeat, using up all the cookies and filling.

Yields 18 pies.

6 tablespoons shortening

1 cup sugar

1 egg

1 cup milk

1 teaspoon vanilla

2 cups flour

1 $^1/_2$ teaspoons baking soda

$^1/_2$ teaspoon salt

$^1/_2$ cup unsweetened cocoa

1 tablespoon oil

Fluffy Vanilla Filling (*recipe below*)

FLUFFY VANILLA FILLING

1. Mix the flour and milk together in a saucepan, and cook over medium heat for 2 to 3 minutes, until thick. Cool well.

2. In the bowl of an electric mixer, cream the butter and shortening together. Add the sugar, salt, and the cooled milk mixture, beating on high speed for 8 minutes, until fluffy. Blend in the vanilla.

Yields 3 cups.

5 tablespoons flour

1 cup milk

$^1/_2$ cup butter, softened

$^1/_2$ cup shortening

1 cup sugar

1 teaspoon salt

1 teaspoon vanilla

2 cups semisweet chocolate chips

³/₄ cup sweetened condensed milk

1 ¹/₂ teaspoons vanilla

pinch salt

1 cup packaged flaked coconut, chopped

CHOCOLATE TRUFFLES

1. Melt the chocolate in the top of a double boiler over simmering water. Remove from the heat and add the condensed milk, vanilla, and salt, stirring until well blended. Chill for 1 hour or until firm enough to handle.

2. Grease your hands with butter and shape the dough into 1" balls. Roll the balls in the coconut. Chill briefly (about 1 hour) before serving.

Yields 36 truffles.

1 cup vanilla wafers, crushed

1 cup confectioners' sugar, sifted

1 ¹/₂ cups pecans, finely chopped

2 tablespoons cocoa

2 tablespoons light corn syrup

¹/₄ cup bourbon

superfine sugar

BOURBON BALLS

1. Mix all the ingredients except the superfine sugar together in a bowl, mixing thoroughly.

2. With your hands and shape the dough into 1" balls. Roll the balls in the superfine sugar. Arrange the balls in a single layer in a plastic dish with a lid. Cover tightly and set aside at least four hours (but preferably overnight) before serving.

Yields 36 balls.

CHOCOLATE COVERED STRAWBERRIES

1 quart strawberries, stems and leaves removed

1 cup (6 ounces) semisweet chocolate bits

1 ¹/₂ teaspoons butter

2 tablespoons milk or light cream

1. Rinse the strawberries in cold water and pat them dry with paper towels.

2. In the top of a double boiler over low heat, melt the chocolate bits with the butter.

3. While the chocolate is melting, heat the milk or light cream in a saucepan over low heat, until warm. When the chocolate is melted, gently stir in the milk or light cream. Thin with more milk if the chocolate remains too thick to dip the strawberries in.

4. Holding the strawberries at the top, dip them in the chocolate, covering about ³/₄ of the berry. Immediately place the strawberries on a chilled plate that has been lightly oiled with vegetable oil, and chill them in the refrigerator until the chocolate has hardened. The strawberries should be served the same day they are made.

Serves 12 to 15.

The Red Lion Inn's birdcage collection in the courtyard.

APPLE HILL DESIGN

1 can (14 ounces) sweetened
   condensed milk

5 ¼ cups (14 ounces) packaged
   flaked coconut

²/₃ cup (two 3-ounce packages)
   strawberry gelatin powder

1 cup blanched almonds, ground

1 teaspoon almond extract

red food coloring

2 ½ cups confectioners' sugar,
   sifted

3 tablespoons cream

green food coloring

STRAWBERRY DELIGHTS

These confections might be used as decorative additions to stemmed glasses of sherbets, ices, ice cream, or in a variety of other ways.

1. Line a baking sheet with parchment or wax paper.

2. Combine the condensed milk, coconut, ¹/₃ cup of the gelatin, almonds, almond extract, and red food coloring in a mixing bowl; stir together well. Cover and chill in the refrigerator until stiff enough to shape, about 1 hour.

3. Divide the dough into half-tablespoon balls, and roll them into strawberry shapes. Roll them in the remaining ¹/₃ cup strawberry gelatin. Place them on the prepared baking sheet.

4. Cream the confectioners' sugar, cream, and green food coloring together in a mixing bowl. Place the mixture in a pastry bag, fitted with a leaf tip, and pipe leaves onto the strawberries. Chill for 1 hour before using them.

Yields 5 dozen.

LET'S HAVE LUNCH AT THE RED LION INN

Just as in Europe, dinner in early New England was eaten at midday, with a much lighter meal in the evening. The practice is still the tradition in much of Europe. Why did we vary the custom?

As farming gave way to industry, as Americans moved to ever-more-distant suburbs, as more housewives took jobs outside the home, as children's schools were located further from home, a large family midday meal became less practical — less possible. Therefore, when the family finally congregated back at the homestead at the end of the day and Mom had time to prepare the evening meal after returning from work herself, that became the time when everyone sat at the table together and shared the day's events.

So we developed a fast-food midday ritual of sandwiches, hamburgers, hot dogs, or items on the school lunch menu, in place of the hearty farm meals of our ancestors. Nevertheless, the leisurely pace of lunch at The Red Lion Inn offers a variety of alternatives, some as hearty as in former days.

New England baked beans, for example, are standard luncheon fare. According to *The American Heritage Cookbook*, "It is for baked beans that Boston is known as Bean Town. The bean pot could be kept in the slow heat of a fireplace to serve at Saturday supper and Sunday breakfast. Housewives too busy with other chores were able to turn the baking of the beans over to a local baker. The baker called each Saturday morning to pick up the family's bean pot and take it to a community oven, usually in the cellar of a nearby tavern. The free-lance baker then returned the baked beans, with a bit of brown bread, on Saturday evening."

Welsh Rarebit is on the Red Lion Inn menu too. It was reputedly improvised when a Welsh gentleman ran out of game for his banquet table and asked his cook to create something new. The cook produced this cheese dish, which he named — presumably to avoid calling the guests' attention to the fact that the meat supply had vanished — "rabbit." It persisted as Welsh Rabbit

According to New England Cookbook, *Welsh Rarebit (or Rabbit, as it is sometimes called by older New England cooks) should be "made from a Cheddar made in June from cow's milk that has in it the sweetness of New England buttercups.... It is not true that a Welsh Rabbit will keep you awake!" Ale or beer was almost always a necessary ingredient, and The Red Lion Inn's version holds true to traditional form.*

in early American kitchens, although generally the name has now been changed to "rarebit."

The Red Lion Inn also offers such comforting lunchtime favorites as chicken pot pie with buttermilk biscuits, roast beef hash, creamed chicken in pastry shells, salmon cakes, and good old fashioned New England corn fritters with fresh-from-the-vat maple syrup. Lunch at The Red Lion Inn is like a trip to grandmother's house, where granny doesn't have to do the work.

Joan Baez drew this sketch in the Red Lion Inn guest book during one of her visits.

WELSH RAREBIT

1. Heat the milk with the bay leaf in a small saucepan.

2. Melt $^1/_4$ cup of the butter in another saucepan. Stir in the flour and cook for 2 to 3 minutes to form a roux. Do not let it brown. Remove the bay leaf from the milk, whisk the milk into the roux, and cook for 6 to 8 minutes, stirring, until thick and creamy. Add the nutmeg.

3. Add the cheese, beer, chicken stock, paprika, tomato paste, Worcestershire sauce, mustard, and salt. Mix thoroughly, and cook slowly over low heat until the cheese has melted, about 5 minutes. Adjust the seasonings to taste. Remove the pan from the heat, cover, and keep warm until you are ready to use it.

4. On a grill, or under the broiler, grill the bacon and the tomato slices until lightly browned. Toast the muffins, and spread them with the remaining $^1/_2$ cup butter. Top each muffin with a slice of bacon and a tomato slice. Pour $^1/_2$ cup of sauce over each rarebit, sprinkle with paprika, and place them under the broiler for 2 minutes, until lightly browned and bubbly. Garnish with chopped parsley, and serve.

Serves 5.

2 cups milk

1 bay leaf

$^3/_4$ cup butter

$^1/_4$ cup flour

$^1/_8$ teaspoon ground nutmeg

2 cups sharp cheddar cheese, grated

$^1/_2$ cup beer

$^1/_2$ cup chicken stock (*see page 38*) or broth

1 teaspoon paprika

$^1/_2$ teaspoon tomato paste

1 teaspoon Worcestershire sauce

$^1/_8$ teaspoon prepared English mustard

salt to taste

10 slices Canadian bacon

10 thick tomato slices

5 English muffins, split

paprika

chopped parsley

4 whole chicken breasts

1 ¹/₂ quarts water

¹/₄ cup white wine

¹/₂ teaspoon dried rosemary

1 clove garlic, crushed

2 small bay leaves

¹/₂ teaspoon leaf thyme

¹/₄ teaspoon leaf tarragon

4 whole black peppercorns

¹/₄ cup clarified butter (*see page 25*)

¹/₄ cup flour

2 carrots, peeled and diced

24 pearl onions

1 cup frozen peas

¹/₄ cup white wine

6 Buttermilk Biscuits, warm (*recipe follows*)

CHICKEN POT PIE

1. Butter six individual crocks or ramekins.

2. Combine the chicken, water, wine, herbs, and peppercorns in a large pot. Bring to a boil over high heat, skimming off any foam that rises to the surface. Reduce the heat and simmer for 20 to 30 minutes, or until the chicken is tender. Remove the chicken from the pot, and let it cool slightly. Remove the skin, and separate the meat from the bones. Set the meat aside and keep it warm.

3. Return the chicken bones to the stock, and simmer until the stock has reduced by half, about 15 minutes. Strain the stock and bring it back to a boil.

4. Over low heat, melt the clarified butter in small saucepan. Stir in the flour, and bring the roux to a slow boil. Cook without browning for 5 minutes. Add this roux to the stock, and simmer for another 10 minutes. Check for taste and adjust the seasonings. Keep the sauce warm.

5. In separate saucepans, cook the carrots and the pearl onions in boiling salted water to cover until just tender, about 8 to 10 minutes for the carrots and 12 to 13 minutes for the onions.

6. Dice the chicken, and toss it with the peas, cooked onions, and carrots. Divide the mixture among six individual crocks or ramekins. Pour the sauce over the chicken, and top with a biscuit. Serve piping hot.

Serves 6.

BUTTERMILK BISCUITS

Any of these biscuits not used immediately can be frozen.

1. Preheat the oven to 400°.

2. Sift the flour, baking powder, and salt together into a bowl. With a pastry blender or two knives, cut in the butter until the mixture has the consistency of small peas.

3. Add the buttermilk and mix it in well with your hands. Form the dough into a ball.

4. On a floured board, roll the dough out to 1/2" thickness. Cut the biscuits out with a biscuit cutter, and arrange them on an ungreased baking sheet. Stir together the egg and water, and brush the biscuits with this wash.

5. Bake at 400° for 25 to 30 minutes, or until golden brown. As soon as you remove the biscuits from the oven, brush them with the melted butter.

Yields 12 biscuits.

1 3/4 cups flour

1 tablespoons + 1 teaspoon baking powder

1/8 teaspoon salt

7 tablespoons butter

1 1/4 cups buttermilk

1 egg

1 tablespoon water

2 tablespoons butter, melted

4 whole chicken breasts, boned and skinned

2 cups chicken stock (*see page 38*) or broth

1 package frozen puff pastry shells

2 tablespoons dry sherry

2 tablespoons sauterne

³/₄ cup red bell peppers, diced

³/₄ cup green bell peppers, diced

¹/₂ cup mushrooms, sliced

¹/₂ cup frozen peas

2 cups Cream Sauce (*recipe below*)

salt and white pepper to taste

2 tablespoons parsley, chopped

¹/₄ cup butter

¹/₄ cup flour

2 cups light cream

2 onions studded with 3 cloves

2 bay leaves

salt and pepper to taste

freshly grated nutmeg to taste

CREAMED CHICKEN RED LION IN PASTRY SHELLS

1. Combine the chicken breasts and the stock in a soup pot, and bring the stock to a boil over high heat. Skim off any foam that rises to the surface. Reduce the heat, and simmer for 15 to 20 minutes, or until the chicken is tender. Remove the chicken from the pot, and allow it to cool. Cut the chicken into medium-sized cubes.

2. Meanwhile, prepare and bake the pastry shells as directed on the package. When they are golden brown and baked, remove them from the oven, and remove the top, setting it aside to use later. Scoop out the doughy inside, and discard it. Then return the hollowed-out shells to the oven for 2 minutes, just long enough to dry out the inside.

3. Combine the wines in a skillet over medium heat, and sauté the peppers and mushrooms in it until they just start to soften, about 4 to 5 minutes. Add the uncooked peas and the chicken, and heat through. Then add the cream sauce; heat but do not boil. Check for seasonings; add salt and pepper to taste.

4. Ladle the creamed chicken over the prepared pastry shells, and place the tops back in place. Garnish with the chopped parsley and serve.

Serves 4.

CREAM SAUCE

1. Melt the butter in a saucepan. Stir in the flour, and cook over low heat for 3 to 4 minutes. Do not brown.

2. In another saucepan, bring the cream just to a boil. Stir the warm cream into the flour mixture, whipping until smooth.

3. Add the onions and bay leaves, and simmer for 20 minutes on low heat. Season with salt, pepper, and nutmeg. Strain the sauce, and serve.

Yields 2 cups.

RED LION INN
LOBSTER CASSEROLE

Coleslaw and roasted potatoes are excellent accompaniments to this dish.

1. Preheat the oven to 350°. Butter a 4-quart ovenproof casserole dish or four individual ramekins.

2. Place the water in a large steamer, and bring it to a boil. Reduce the heat to bring the water to a simmer. Place the lobsters, salt, parsley stems, and Old Bay seasoning in the steamer, and cook for 12 to 15 minutes, or until the lobster shells turns red and the meat is cooked.

3. Clean and cut up the lobsters, removing the tail, claw, and leg meat. Split the tail meat in half, and then cut each half into 6 pieces. Leave the claw meat whole but remove the cartilage. There should be approximately 1 cup of meat from each lobster.

4. Place the lobster meat in the prepared casserole or ramekins, and drizzle $^1/_4$ cup of the sherry over the top.

5. Melt $^1/_2$ cup of the butter. In a small bowl, combine the remaining $^1/_4$ cup of sherry, $^1/_4$ cup of the melted butter, the bread crumbs, $^1/_4$ cup of the parsley, the thyme, and the ketchup. Mix well and sprinkle this mixture over the lobster (do not pat it down).

6. Dot the remaining $^1/_4$ cup unmelted butter over the bread crumb mixture. Bake at 350° for 12 to 15 minutes, until bubbly hot.

7. Meanwhile, cut the crusts off the bread, and toast the slices. Cut the toast in half to form triangles, and butter them with the remaining $^1/_4$ cup melted butter. Dip the tips in the paprika. Dip the tips of the lemon wedges in the remaining 4 teaspoons chopped parsley.

8. Serve the lobster, accompanied by the toast and lemon wedges.

Serves 4.

2 cups water

4 lobsters (about 1 $^1/_2$ pounds each)

2 teaspoons salt

4 teaspoons parsley stems, chopped

4 tablespoons Old Bay seasoning

$^1/_2$ cup dry sherry

$^3/_4$ cup butter

1 cup dried bread crumbs

$^1/_4$ cup plus 4 teaspoons parsley, chopped

$^1/_2$ teaspoon dried thyme

4 teaspoons ketchup

8 slices white bread

4 teaspoons paprika

1 pound angel hair pasta

water to cover pasta

3 tablespoons olive oil

3 cloves garlic, finely chopped

1 head broccoli, separated into flowerets (reserve the stems for another use)

2 red bell peppers, diced

2 cups heavy cream

1 cup Parmesan cheese, grated

$1/8$ teaspoon ground nutmeg

salt and pepper to taste

Parmesan cheese, for serving

Angel Hair Pasta with Stir-Fried Broccoli

1. Cook the pasta in boiling, salted water for 4 to 6 minutes, or until just tender. Drain the pasta and toss it with 1 tablespoon of the oil to keep it from sticking together, then keep it warm.

2. Heat the remaining 2 tablespoons olive oil in a skillet. Add the garlic and sauté it lightly; do not brown. Add the broccoli flowerets and peppers, and sauté over medium heat until tender, about 5 to 7 minutes. Remove the vegetables from the skillet.

3. Add the cream to the pan and bring to a boil. Reduce the heat and simmer until it starts to thicken, about 5 minutes. Add the Parmesan cheese and nutmeg, and cook an additional 2 minutes to thicken it a bit more. Add the vegetables and the cooked pasta. Toss them together well. Season with salt and pepper if needed. Serve immediately, with additional Parmesan on the side.

Serves 8.

CORN FRITTERS

Corn and maple syrup are the essence of New England. When the sugar houses in northern Berkshire County start their production of maple syrup in early March, many of them open makeshift breakfast halls, where they serve pancakes and corn fritters with fresh maple syrup, direct from the vat. Is there anything sweeter? Outside the sugar shacks, the line in the snappy cold is often several country blocks long. Inside, the chairs are made from sawn logs, and the tables, set family-style, are made from huge slabs of maple. At The Red Lion Inn, you can dine on the same corn fritters with fresh maple syrup and Red Lion Inn Breakfast Sausage (*see page 182*), in a more refined atmosphere — and they're every bit as good.

1. Heat a deep fryer filled with vegetable oil to 325°.

2. Combine the corns in a mixing bowl. Separate the eggs and add the yolks to the corn, mixing well.

3. In another bowl, whip the egg whites to form soft peaks. Add the salt and continue to whip until they reach the stiff peak stage.

4. Add the milk to the corn mixture; then add the flour and baking powder, and sugar, and mix them all together well. Fold in the beaten egg whites.

5. Using a small ice cream scoop, drop scoops of dough into the hot fat and fry at 325° until golden brown and cooked completely. Remove the fritters from the fat and drain on paper towels. Dust with the confectioners' sugar. Serve the fritters with maple syrup.

Serves 8 to 10.

1 1/2 cups whole-kernel corn

1 1/2 cups canned creamed corn

5 eggs

1/4 teaspoon salt

1/3 cup milk

1 1/2 cups flour

1 tablespoons baking powder

1/3 cup sugar

confectioners' sugar, for dusting

maple syrup, for serving

1 pound yellow eye or navy beans

1/2 cup yellow onions, diced

1 pound salt pork

1 pound Black Forest ham, cooked and diced

1/2 cup dark molasses

1/3 cup ketchup

1 teaspoon salt

1/2 teaspoon dry mustard

2 tablespoons dark brown sugar

Red Lion Inn Applesauce (*recipe follows*)

*"Long ago, at the end of the route,
The stage pulled up, and the folks stepped out.
They have all passed under the tavern door —
The youth and his bride and the gray three-score.
Their eyes were weary with dust and gleam,
The day had gone like an empty dream.
Soft may they slumber, and trouble no more
For their eager journey, its jolt and roar,
In the old coach over the mountain."*

Old Tavern Song

Boston Baked Beans with Black Forest Ham, Brown Bread, and Applesauce

1. Pick over the beans, discarding any impurities. Rinse them thoroughly, until the water runs clear. Place the beans in an earthenware bean pot, cover with cold water, and let them soak for 4 to 6 hours, or overnight.

2. Preheat the oven to 325°. Without draining them, put the beans over medium heat and bring the water to a boil. Cover the pot and simmer the beans for 30 minutes.

3. Add the onions to the beans. Score the salt pork into wedges, cutting through the lean meat but not the rind. Add the salt pork and the cubed ham to the beans. Combine the molasses, ketchup, salt, mustard, and brown sugars in a small bowl. Stir them well, and then add the mixture to the beans. Bring to a boil.

4. Cover the pot and transfer it to the oven. Bake in a 325° oven for 6 to 8 hours, until done, watching that the beans don't get too dry. If necessary, add more water (keep the water at the level of the beans). Uncover the pot for the last 30 minutes of cooking to brown the beans. Serve with brown bread and applesauce.

Serves 6.

RED LION INN APPLESAUCE

1. Rinse the apples well, and cut them into quarters (do not peel them). Remove the core and seeds.

2. Put the apples in a roomy saucepan, and add 1" water. Cover tightly and bring to a boil. Simmer for about 40 minutes, until tender and soft, being careful they don't burn.

3. Add the sugars and spices to the apples. Cover and simmer for 10 minutes, until all the sugar has dissolved.

4. Pass the apple mixture through a food processor or a food mill fitted with a fine blade. Serve warm or chilled.

Serves 6.

10 large McIntosh apples

$^1/_2$ cup light brown sugar, firmly packed

$^1/_2$ cup granulated sugar

1 tablespoon ground cinnamon

1 tablespoon ground nutmeg

The Country Curtains shop at The Red Lion Inn.

COUNTRY LION AGENCY

4 quarts water

1 teaspoon salad oil

$^1/_2$ teaspoon salt

3 cups (8 ounces) dry medium-sized macaroni shells

$^1/_2$ cup butter

$^1/_4$ cup sliced blanched almonds

2 tablespoons shallots, minced

1 pound small shrimp, cleaned, peeled, and deveined

$^1/_3$ cup amaretto liqueur

3 cups heavy cream

$^1/_8$ teaspoon cayenne pepper

salt and white pepper to taste

1 cup frozen peas

$^1/_4$ cup parsley, chopped

Pasta Shells with Shrimp, Peas, and Amaretto Cream Sauce

1. Bring the water to a rapid boil. Add the oil, salt, and shells. Cook the pasta for 10 to 12 minutes, until just tender.

2. Melt $^1/_4$ cup of the butter in a sauté pan. Add the almonds and sauté for 2 minutes over low heat, until light golden brown. Do not allow them to scorch. Drain and set aside.

3. Melt the remaining $^1/_4$ cup butter in another sauté pan. Add the shallots and sauté over medium heat for 2 minutes. Add the shrimp and sauté for 4 to 6 minutes, until pink and cooked through.

4. Add the amaretto and then the cream to the pan. Bring to a boil and simmer for 8 minutes, or until the sauce is thick and creamy. Add the cayenne, salt, white pepper, and peas, and heat for 1 minute. Remove from the heat.

5. Add the cooked pasta and toss all together. Garnish each serving with sauted almonds and parsley.

Serves 4.

NEW ENGLAND SALMON CAKES WITH CREAMY CELERY SAUCE

1. Prepare a court-bouillon: Tie the pickling spices up in a cheesecloth bag. Combine the parsley stems, white wine, lemon slice, spice bag, and water in a large saucepan. Bring to a boil and simmer for 10 to 12 minutes.

2. Place the salmon in the court-bouillon and simmer for approximately 12 minutes, or until it flakes when prodded with a fork. Transfer the salmon from the bouillon to a large mixing bowl, and flake it thoroughly with a fork. You should have about 2 cups flaked salmon.

3. Stir the eggs into the salmon. Add the cracker crumbs and all the remaining ingredients through the sherry. Mix together well. Cover and chill for 1 hour or longer.

4. Form the salmon mixture into 18 patties. Heat the butter in a large skillet, and sauté the patties over medium heat until golden brown and cooked through, about 5 minutes on each side.

5. Spoon some of the Creamy Celery Sauce over the salmon cakes, and pass the rest separately.

Serves 4.

1 tablespoon pickling spice

2 tablespoons parsley stems, chopped

$1/2$ cup white wine

1 lemon slice

2 cups water

1 $1/2$ pounds salmon

2 eggs, beaten

$1/2$ cup Ritz crackers, finely crushed

$1/2$ teaspoon salt

$1/8$ teaspoon paprika

$1/4$ teaspoon garlic powder

$1/2$ teaspoon onion powder

2 tablespoons parsley, chopped

$1/4$ teaspoon Worcestershire sauce

2 drops Tabasco sauce

1 teaspoon dry sherry

2 tablespoons butter

Creamy Celery Sauce (*recipe follows*)

2 bunches celery

1 medium onion

4 cups water

$1/2$ teaspoon garlic powder

2 tablespoons dry white wine

1 tablespoon dry sherry

1 or 2 drops Tabasco sauce

$1/2$ cup butter

$1/2$ cup flour

$1/4$ cup heavy cream

1 teaspoon white pepper

CREAMY CELERY SAUCE

1. Peel any woody strings from the celery and chop it into medium-sized pieces. Peel the onion and chop it into medium-sized pieces, and cook both vegetables in separate saucepans of boiling salted water deep enough to cover them, until tender. Remove the vegetables from the pans, reserving the water. Puree the vegetables in a food processor or a blender in batches. You should have 2 cups celery puree and $1/4$ cup onion puree.

2. Combine the vegetable purees, water (you should use the reserved vegetable water), garlic powder, white wine, sherry, and Tabasco in a saucepan and simmer for 45 minutes.

3. Make a roux by melting the butter in a small saucepan. Stir in the flour and cook for 2 to 3 minutes. Whisk the roux into the celery mixture, and simmer for 10 minutes. Skim off any foam that comes to the surface.

4. Taste for salt, although none should be needed. Add the heavy cream and pepper, and heat but do not boil.

5. Serve over salmon cakes with extra sauce on the side.

Yields 4 cups.

SEAFOOD CRÊPES

1. Preheat the oven to 325°. Butter a 7" x 11" casserole dish.

2. Place the scallops, shrimp, and fish in a large steamer, over simmering water. Steam the seafood until it is tender, about 10 minutes.

3. To the prepared Cream Sauce, add the sherry, and then stir in salt, pepper, and paprika. Add the seafood and cook 1 to 2 minutes to coat with the sauce.

4. Place approximately $^1/_8$ cup of the seafood and sauce in the center of each crêpe and roll them up, encasing the filling. Place the crêpes side by side in the prepared casserole dish. Pour $^1/_2$ cup of the Seafood Newburg Sauce over the crêpes. Bake at 325° for 8 to 10 minutes, or until hot and bubbly.

5. Serve two crêpes per person, with additional Seafood Newburg Sauce on the side.

Serves 5 to 6.

$^1/_2$ **pound scallops, diced**

$^1/_2$ **pound small shrimp, cleaned, peeled, and deveined**

$^1/_2$ **pound haddock, cod, sole, or any firm white fish, diced**

2 cups Cream Sauce (*see page 166*)

$^1/_4$ **cup sherry**

salt and pepper to taste

1 teaspoon paprika

10 to 12 crêpes (*recipe follows*)

Seafood Newburg Sauce (*recipe follows*)

2 eggs, room temperature

1 ¼ cups milk, room temperature

1 cup flour

¼ teaspoon salt

¼ cup clarified butter (*see page 25*)

CRÊPES

1. Whip the eggs in a stainless steel bowl until thoroughly beaten.

2. Add the milk, flour, salt, and clarified butter, and whip until smooth. Let the batter rest, covered, for 1 hour to release the air bubbles.

3. Lightly oil a well-seasoned crêpe or small omelet pan, and heat it over moderate heat. Drop about ⅛ cup of the batter into the pan, and quickly tilt the pan to evenly coat the bottom. The batter should be thin and even, with no holes or gaps. Cook gently 1 to 2 minutes, until lightly browned on the edges. Turn the crêpe over and cook 1 more minute.

4. As they are cooked, stack the crêpes on a platter and keep them warm in the oven. These crêpes may be made a day ahead, and wrapped tightly in plastic wrap. Warm slightly to facilitate separating, when ready to use.

Yields 18 to 22 crêpes.

2 tablespoons butter

2 teaspoons shallots, minced

2 tablespoons paprika

½ cup dry sherry

2 tablespoons tomato paste

2 tablespoons brandy

2 cups Cream Sauce (*see page 166*)

⅛ teaspoon dried thyme

pinch cayenne pepper

SEAFOOD NEWBURG SAUCE

1. Melt the butter in a sauté pan. Add the shallots and sauté over medium heat for 2 to 3 minutes, until translucent. Add the paprika and sherry, and sauté for 2 minutes. Stir in the tomato paste.

2. Add the brandy to the sauté pan, and carefully light it with a match. When the alcohol has burned off, add the cream sauce, thyme, and cayenne. Cook for 2 minutes more.

Yields 2 ½ cups.

RED LION INN BEEF STEW

1. Trim the beef and cut it into ³/₄ to 1" cubes. Place the flour in a shallow dish, and season it with salt and pepper. Dredge the meat in the seasoned flour, shaking off any excess.

2. In a heavy Dutch oven, heat enough oil to cover the bottom by ¹/₄". Add the beef and sauté over medium-high heat until well browned, 10 to 12 minutes. Add the diced onions and sauté for another 8 to 10 minutes, until the onions are browned and very lightly caramelized.

3. Add the beef stock, stirring well with a wooden spoon, and scraping the bottom of the pan. Bring to a boil and simmer for 35 to 40 minutes. Add the tomatoes, herbs, Worcestershire sauce, wine, and bay leaves. Simmer gently for another 30 minutes.

4. Bring the water to a boil in another pot. Add the salt and the potatoes and carrots, and cook for 3 minutes. Then add the celery and the pearl onions and cook another 7 to 9 minutes, until the vegetables are just tender. Add the peas and cook an additional 2 minutes.

5. Drain the vegetables, and add them to the beef stew. Simmer the stew for 5 minutes. Taste for salt and pepper. Remove the bay leaf, and serve.

Serves 10 to 12.

2 pounds beef stew meat

¹/₃ cup flour

salt and pepper

¹/₂ cup vegetable oil

2 cups onions (about 1 ¹/₄ pounds), cut into 1 ¹/₂" cubes

6 cups beef stock (*see page 37*) or broth

1 ¹/₂ cups canned tomatoes, diced

1 tablespoon dried oregano

1 ¹/₄ tablespoons dried basil

1 ¹/₂ teaspoons garlic powder

1 teaspoon Worcestershire sauce

¹/₂ cup red burgundy wine

2 bay leaves

4 quarts water

1 teaspoon salt

2 cups potatoes (about 1 pound), peeled and cut into 1¹/₂" cubes

²/₃ cup carrots, peeled and cut into ¹/₂" cubes

1 ¹/₂ cups celery (about 10 ounces), trimmed and cut into ¹/₂" cubes

¹/₂ cup tiny pearl onions

¹/₂ cup frozen peas

salt and pepper to taste

A RED LION INN
BREAKFAST

When Calvin Coolidge, a native of Massachusetts and a frequent visitor to The Red Lion Inn, was in the White House, he insisted on continuing his New England breakfasts, which consisted of a hot cereal made from unground wheat and rye, and corn muffins made according to an old New England recipe.

Traditional New England corn muffins are available today at The Red Lion Inn, as they have been for many years. Pancakes and various egg dishes are available as well. James Beard in *American Cookery* remarked, "I'm sure we lead the world, as we always have, on the subject of breakfast eggs. Our variety of egg and meat combinations for this meal is unequaled when we begin to tally ham and eggs, and sausage, meat or link, and eggs. And we are the only country I can think of where potatoes are important as a breakfast food — hashed brown or country-fried or cottage fried potatoes — combined with eggs, or meat and eggs."

One of the most enduringly popular breakfast treats at The Red Lion Inn, however, is old-fashioned oatmeal, served steaming hot with brown sugar and raisins. Popular variations offer oatmeal served with chopped dates and maple syrup, or with bananas and honey, or with dried apples added just before serving. The popularity of oatmeal probably stems from the fact that The Red Lion Inn is one of the few restaurants remaining that serves oatmeal at all. It's a lasting reminder of the timelessness of The Red Lion Inn.

"Yet, who can help loving the land that has taught us
*　　Six hundred and eighty-five ways to dress eggs?"*

Thomas Moore 1779-1852, The Fudge Family in Paris

BERKSHIRE APPLE PANCAKE

This popular Red Lion Inn recipe uses two products from the bounty of the Berkshires — apples and maple syrup.

1. Preheat the oven to 450°.

2. Peel and core the apples. Coarsely chop 2 1/2 of the apples. Slice the remaining 1/2 apple into thin spirals for garnish on top. Brush the spirals with lemon juice to prevent them from darkening, and set them aside.

3. Mix the eggs, flour, baking powder, salt, sugar, milk, vanilla, cinnamon, and the chopped apples together in a bowl. Beat until they are combined, although the batter will remain lumpy.

4. Melt the butter in a 10" cast iron frying pan. Pour the batter into the pan, and arrange the reserved apple spirals on top.

5. Bake the pancake in the oven at 450° for 15 minutes. Then turn the oven down to 350° and continue to bake the pancake an additional 40 minutes, or until a toothpick inserted in the center comes out clean. Remove the pan from the oven and allow it to rest for 5 minutes.

6. Sprinkle the brown sugar over the top of the pancake, cut into wedges, and serve with the warm maple syrup.

Serves 6.

3 apples

3 eggs, beaten

3 cups flour

1 1/2 tablespoons baking powder

3/4 teaspoon salt

5 tablespoons sugar

2 cups milk

3/4 teaspoon vanilla

3/4 teaspoon ground cinnamon

5 tablespoons butter, melted

1/4 cup light brown sugar, firmly packed

warm maple syrup, for serving

"I said my prayers and ate some cranberry tart for breakfast."

From the dairy of William Byrd, 1711

4 eggs

$^1/_2$ cup milk

1 teaspoon ground cinnamon

$^1/_2$ teaspoon vanilla

$^3/_4$ teaspoon honey

1 tablespoon granulated sugar

16 slices Challah (*see page 76*)

confectioners' sugar

warm maple syrup, for serving

FRENCH TOAST

For an added taste treat, substitute bourbon for the vanilla in this recipe.

1. Preheat a griddle to 325°. Oil the griddle.

2. Beat the eggs, milk, cinnamon, vanilla, honey, and granulated sugar together in a bowl.

3. Dip each slice of Challah in the egg mixture, and then grill it for 4 to 5 minutes on each side, until golden brown.

4. Sprinkle the French toast with confectioners' sugar, and serve with warm maple syrup on the side.

Serves 4.

Buttermilk Pancakes with Blueberries

At The Red Lion Inn, breakfast pancakes are often served with berries or fruits in season. That might mean strawberries, blueberries, apples, or even bananas.

1. Preheat a griddle to medium heat. Lightly oil the griddle.

2. Rinse the blueberries thoroughly, and remove the stems, any shrunken berries, and impurities.

3. Whip the eggs and buttermilk together in a large bowl.

4. Combine all the dry ingredients in a separate bowl, then add to the buttermilk mixture. Add the melted shortening and mix well, but *do not overmix.* Keep the mixture somewhat lumpy.

5. Using a $1/4$ cup ladle, pour the batter onto the prepared griddle. Sprinkle 1 tablespoon of the blueberries on top of each pancake. Cook until bubbles appear on top, about 3 to 4 minutes. Turn over and cook 2 to 3 minutes on the other side.

6. Serve with warm maple syrup.

Serves 6 to 8.

1 pint blueberries (or other fruit in season)

7 eggs

2 cups buttermilk

2 $1/2$ cups flour

1 $1/2$ teaspoons baking soda

1 $1/2$ teaspoons salt

4 $1/2$ teaspoons baking powder

1 tablespoon shortening, melted

warm maple syrup, for serving

ART MARASCO

The front porch of The Red Lion Inn.

6 pounds boneless pork butt,
    trimmed of sinew and gristle

$1/4$ cup salt

$1/4$ cup ground sage

1 $1/2$ tablespoons cayenne pepper

1 $1/2$ tablespoons light brown sugar,
    firmly packed

RED LION INN
BREAKFAST SAUSAGE

If you won't be cooking this sausage within twenty-four hours of preparing it, store it in the freezer. It will keep frozen for up to three months.

1. Cut the pork, along with its fat, into 1" cubes.

2. Stir the seasonings together, and toss well with the pork. Cover and chill overnight.

3. In a well-chilled meat grinder with a $1/8$" blade, grind the sausage once (for a coarse, country-style sausage). Shape into patties; or roll the meat up in parchment paper to form a cylinder, and slice $1/2$" thick. Pan-grill or broil, as desired.

Yields 6 pounds.

OLD-FASHIONED OATMEAL

Popular Red Lion Inn variations include oatmeal served with chopped dates and maple syrup, or with bananas and honey, or with dried apples.

1. Combine the oatmeal, water, milk, and salt in a large saucepan, and bring to a boil. Cook slowly for 5 minutes. Remove from the heat and allow to stand until it has reached the desired consistency (it will thicken as it stands).

2. Sprinkle the oatmeal with sugar and raisins, and serve.

Serves 6.

2 cups old-fashioned oatmeal (stone ground, if available)

3 cups cold water

1 cup cold milk

$^1/_4$ teaspoon salt

2 tablespoons light brown sugar

1 tablespoon brown raisins

"The critical period in matrimony is breakfast-time."

A. P. Herbert

12 eggs

$^1/_2$ cup clarified butter (*see page 25*)

12 slices smoked salmon

$^1/_2$ cup sour cream

2 tablespoons + 2 teaspoons fresh
dill, chopped

4 sprigs fresh dill

4 teaspoons salmon caviar

SALMON OMELET WITH SOUR CREAM, DILL, AND SALMON CAVIAR

1. With a wire whisk, beat the eggs in a stainless steel or glass bowl until foamy.

2. Melt 2 tablespoons of the clarified butter in an omelet pan over moderate heat. Pour $^1/_4$ of the eggs into the pan. As the eggs begin to set, roll pan from side to side, covering the bottom. When it is set on the bottom, flip the omelet over. Lay 3 slices of the smoked salmon, 1 tablespoon of the sour cream, and 1 teaspoon of the chopped dill on top.

3. When the omelet is set on the second side, roll or fold it in half. Remove it from the heat and place on a warmed plate. Slit the top of the omelet and spoon 1 tablespoon more of the sour cream into the slit. Sprinkle caviar over the sour cream, and top with a large dill sprig.

4. Repeat three times, with the remaining ingredients.

Serves 4.

RED LION INN HOME FRIES

1. Cook the potatoes in a vegetable steamer over simmering water for 20 to 30 minutes, until just tender.

2. Melt the butter in a heavy skillet, and add the onions and 1 tablespoon of the seasoning mix. Sauté over medium heat until the onions are limp and translucent, about 10 minutes. Do not let them brown. Add the potatoes, and sprinkle with the remaining 1 tablespoon seasoning mix. Sauté over medium heat until golden brown and crisp, about 15 minutes. Dot with more butter for added flavor.

Serves 8.

2 pounds potatoes, peeled and diced into $^1/_4$" cubes

1 cup butter

$^3/_4$ cup onions, diced

2 tablespoons Home Fries Seasoning Mix (*recipe below*)

butter, for serving (optional)

HOME FRIES SEASONING MIX

Chef Mongeon uses this seasoning mix for a variety of dishes. He sprinkles it over roasted potatoes, or rubs it into the skin of a chicken before roasting it, as well as using it as a seasoning for Red Lion Inn Home Fries.

1. Combine all the ingredients in a large jar or other covered container. Shake to mix well. This will last up to six months.

Yields 3 cups.

1 cup salt

$^1/_2$ cup paprika

$^1/_4$ cup ground black pepper

$^1/_4$ cup ground white pepper

$^1/_2$ cup onion powder

$^1/_2$ cup garlic salt

2 English muffins

¹/₄ cup butter

2 quarts water

4 eggs

4 slices Canadian bacon

Hollandaise Sauce (*see page 82*)

4 black olives, sliced

¹/₄ cup parsley, chopped

EGGS BENEDICT WITH CANADIAN BACON

This recipe may be varied by substituting smoked salmon slices for the Canadian bacon, a dill Hollandaise Sauce for the regular Hollandaise, salmon roe for the black olives, and a sprig of dill for the parsley.

1. Split the English muffins, toast them, and spread them with the butter. Place them in a warm oven to keep them warm and crisp.

2. Bring the water to a slow, easy simmer in a shallow saucepan. Crack the eggs, one at a time, into a cup or saucer, and then slide them into the poaching water. Poach for 5 to 8 minutes, until cooked to your taste.

3. Meanwhile grill the Canadian bacon slices, and place one on each English muffin half. Remove the eggs from the water with a slotted spoon, and drain them. Trim the edges with kitchen shears or a knife, if you like, to remove irregular edges. Place a poached egg on top of each muffin, and spoon Hollandaise Sauce on top. Garnish with sliced black olives and some chopped parsley.

Serves 2.

Red Lion Inn Roast Beef Hash

1. Trim the fat and gristle from the beef, and cut it into 1" cubes. Peel and quarter the onions.

2. Combine the meat, potatoes, onions, and seasonings in a large bowl, and mix thoroughly. Set aside, covered, to mellow for 2 hours.

3. Using a food processor or a meat grinder, coarsely dice or chop the meat mixture, but do not allow it to get mushy.

4. Heat the oil in a heavy skillet, and cook the hash over medium heat, until the potatoes are brown. Turn the hash over and grill the other side. Adjust the seasonings to taste.

5. While the hash is cooking, fry or poach the eggs. Top each portion of hash with two eggs, and serve with ketchup on the side.

Serves 6.

1 1/4 pounds cooked prime rib or roast beef

1/2 pound onions

3/4 pound potatoes, peeled, cooked, and diced

1/2 teaspoon salt

1/2 teaspoon black pepper

1 teaspoon dried thyme

1 teaspoon garlic powder

1/2 teaspoon dried marjoram

1 tablespoon Worcestershire sauce

1/4 cup vegetable oil

12 eggs

ketchup, for serving

Mrs. Harriet Martineau, author of Society in America, *1837, and* Retrospect of Western Travel, *1838, stayed in Stockbridge, probably at The Red Lion Inn, and noted that she breakfasted on "excellent bread, potatoes, hung beef, eggs and strong tea at Stockbridge, Mass."*

When The Red Lion Inn sought a liquor license in 1934 after 95 dry years, a sometime local resident penned this poem:

Yes, ninety-five long years have passed
Since first mine host, Pepoon,
Regarding well his pots and pans
And platters, knives and spoon.

While Bingham, Kingsley, and John Hicks
In order passed along;
And at the corner of the Inn
A haughty lion hung.

Red was his color, and his name,
He braved the summer's heat
The winter's cold, with ice and snow
That never chilled his feet.
Then Kingsley, Rockwell, Gilpin, Plumb,
Pilling and Heaton, too—
What hosts they were, as fine a lot
As e're one ever knew.

And not a dram of liquor served,
No, not one tiny drop.
A thirst that must be satisfied
Must seek another shop.

Red Lion Inn was dry forsooth
In rafter and in mood,
And in the wee small hours of night
Would crack and creak and brood;—

(continued on next page)

COCKTAILS AND DRINKS

In the early days, a tavern's prosperity depended chiefly on the warmth of its log fire and the fire in its punch. The following description quoted in *Stage-Coach and Tavern Days* demonstrates the importance of tavern libations: "A man can never make good punch unless he is satisfied, nay positive, that no man breathing can make better. I retire to a solitary corner with my ingredients ready sorted; they are as follows, and I mix them in the order they are here written. Sugar, twelve tolerable lumps; hot water, one pint; lemons, two, the juice and peel; old Jamaica rum, two gills; brandy, one gill; porter or stout, half a gill; arrack, a slight dash. I allow myself five minutes to make a bowl in the foregoing proportions, carefully stirring the mixture as I furnish the ingredients until it actually foams; and then Kangaroos! How beautiful it is!"

Flips were warm winter drinks, heated by thrusting an iron flip dog (firepoker) into the mug, which produced a sizzle and a burnt taste. According to *The American Heritage Cookbook*, a frequent early traveler, Myles Arnold, insisted the flip was especially popular with the riders on the Boston Post route: "and indeed, 'tis said they sometimes wrap themselves warmly with it."

When Silas Pepoon owned The Red Lion Inn, tavern parties were festive affairs. Accounts claim there was dancing and merrymaking among the young people. The ladies sipped wine and cider and a headier drink, the flip, while the gentlemen indulged in even more fiery and exciting beverages. When parties were not going on, Pepoon handed out hot punches and rum toddies over the bar in the public room and lamented the horrible condition of the roads (the west end of Main Street had a way of disappearing under water when the meadows flooded).

According to Eleanor Early in her *New England Cookbook*, cider was a staple of the early tavern bar. New Englanders had been making hard cider since well before the Revolution, as a way to use up some of the apples their trees produced. Even today, a crock of steaming cider is ready for guests at The Lion's Den, the downstairs "pub" at The Red Lion Inn.

Cheap molasses from the West Indies created the highly profitable New England rum industry, which played such an important role in early trade. According to historian Samuel Eliot Morison, "The West Indies trade was the main factor in New England prosperity until the American Revolution; without it the settlements on the northern coast would have remained stationary or declined." Once they began importing molasses, rum, or "Kill Devil," became the drink of preference in taverns.

Rum drinks are still popular at The Red Lion Inn, including a smooth hot buttered rum, and a holiday eggnog. The hot spiced cider is the perfect warmer-upper after a day on the nearby ski slopes.

O'er juleps, punches, stirrup cups,
And ale, upon the draught,
With spirits in that hostelry
To promulgate its craft.
And thoughts symbolic of its sign
So bold, (just stop and think),
A Lion, and e'en Red at that,
And not a drop to drink.

But times have changed since old Pepoon
In his good ways was set,
For in the race to hold the pace
The Inn is going "wet,"

Ye shades of Bingham, Plumb and Hicks,
Kingsley and Heaton too,
What kind of punch, of widespread fame,
Will the "Red Lion" brew?

Edward P. Merwin

1 ¼ ounces brandy

¾ cup milk, chilled

1 teaspoon sugar

ground nutmeg

BRANDY MILK PUNCH

1. Combine the first three ingredients in a container, add some shaved ice, and shake. Strain into a chilled collins glass, and sprinkle the nutmeg on top.

Serves 1.

1 lump sugar

1 piece cinnamon stick, 1 ½" long

2 whole cloves

¾ cup boiling water

1 teaspoon butter

1 ¼ ounce dark rum

1 teaspoon maple syrup

ground nutmeg

HOT BUTTERED RUM

1. Put the sugar, cinnamon stick, and cloves in a heated mug and add the boiling water. Add the butter, rum, and maple syrup; and stir. Sprinkle with nutmeg.

Serves 1.

1 lump sugar

¾ cup boiling water

1 cinnamon stick, 1 ½" long

3 whole cloves

1 ¼ ounce blended whiskey

slice of lemon

HOT TODDY

1. Dissolve the sugar in the boiling water in a heated mug. Add the cinnamon, cloves, and whiskey, and stir. Garnish with the lemon slice.

Serves 1.

Hot Spiced Cider

This drink is equally popular at The Red Lion Inn without the rum, as a hot non-alcoholic drink.

1. Pour all the ingredients except the nutmeg into a heated mug. Let steep 3 minutes, stir, and then sprinkle with the nutmeg.

Serves 1.

1 ¼ ounces dark rum

1 orange peel

1 cinnamon stick, 1 ½" long

2 whole cloves

6 ounces apple cider, heated

dash of ground nutmeg

Fitz Irish Coffee

1. Put the Kahlua into a heated mug or stemmed goblet. Add the whiskey and hot coffee, and stir. Add a dollop of whipped cream, and sprinkle with nutmeg.

Serves 1.

1 ounce Kahlua liqueur

1 ounce Irish whiskey

1 cup hot black coffee

fresh whipped cream

ground nutmeg

Holiday Eggnog

1. Shake the first four ingredients in a container with some shaved ice, and strain into a large chilled wine glass. Sprinkle with nutmeg.

Serves 1.

1 ¼ ounces dark rum

1 egg

1 teaspoon sugar

½ cup milk, chilled

ground nutmeg

1 ounce gin

6 tablespoons orange juice

6 tablespoons lemon juice

2 drops grenadine

club soda, chilled

BINGHAM'S BLUSH

This delightful libation is named after the cozy Widow Bingham's Tavern at The Red Lion Inn.

1. Shake the gin, juices, and grenadine in a container, add some shaved ice, and shake vigorously. Strain over ice into a collins glass, and fill the glass with club soda.

Serves 1.

PHOTO COURTESY OF THE NORMAN ROCKWELL MUSEUM AT STOCKBRIDGE. PHOTO BY LOUIE LAMONE.

John Wayne and Norman Rockwell.

PIÑA COLADA

This drink is one of the all-time favorites at The Red Lion Inn, especially when sipped in the summer courtyard, next to the lion statue.

1. Put all the ingredients except the pineapple into a blender. Blend at high speed for 15 seconds. Pour into a hurricane glass and garnish with the pineapple.

Serves 1.

1 $^1/_2$ ounces light rum

6 tablespoons pineapple juice

4 tablespoons coconut cream

$^3/_4$ cup ice

1 piece fresh pineapple, for garnish

BLOODY MARY

The Bloody Marys at The Red Lion Inn have been justifiably renowned for years. They are made with fresh ingredients, and each is individually prepared — no mixes used here!

1. Combine the vodka, lemon juice, and seasonings in a hurricane glass. Stir well. Add a stalk of celery, and a wedge of lime.

Serves 1.

1 ounce vodka

$^3/_4$ cup tomato juice

2 dashes lemon juice

4 dashes Worcestershire sauce

2 to 3 drops Tabasco sauce

2 dashes salt and pepper

$^1/_4$ teaspoon horseradish (optional)

fresh celery stick, for garnish

lime wedge, for garnish

2 quarts red wine

1 pint sweet vermouth

15 whole cloves

2 cinnamon sticks, 3" long

2 ounces dried orange peel

20 cardamom seeds, crushed

1 ½ cups blanched almonds

1 ½ cups raisins

½ pound lump sugar

1 cup vodka

Benjamin Franklin's Orange Shrub

"To a Gallon of Rum two Quarts of Orange Juice and two pound of Sugar — dissolve the Sugar in the Juice before you mix it with the Rum — put all together in a Cask & shake it well — let it stand 3 or 4 weeks and it will be very fine & fit for Bottling — when you have Bottled off the fine pass the thick thro' a Philtring paper put into a Funnell — that not a drop may be lost. To obtain the flavour of the Orange Peel paire a few Oranges & put it in Rum for twelve hours — & put that Rum into the Cask with the other — For Punch thought better without the Peel."

The Franklin Papers, *American Philosophical Society*

THE RED LION INN
CHRISTMAS DRINK GLÖOG

The holiday season is always festive and colorful at The Red Lion Inn, where corporations and individuals host private parties. This holiday drink was created just for this special season.

1. Put all the ingredients except sugar and vodka in a saucepan and boil slowly for 20 minutes, stirring occasionally. Place a rack over the pan, and spread the sugar lumps out on it.

2. Warm the vodka in a small saucepan, and pour it over the sugar lumps, saturating them. Carefully ignite the sugar, and let it melt into the glöog mixture. Stir.

3. Strain into heated mugs or punch cups, and add a few of the cooked almonds and raisins to each cup. (Leftover glöog can be bottled and reheated.)

Serves 10.

Children are an important part of the hospitality scene at The Red Lion Inn, so it's not surprising that special drinks have been created just for them. Standards like "Shirley Temples" are served at the inn, but so are the following:

Fitz Fizz

2 tablespoons lemon juice

2 tablespoons pineapple juice

2 tablespoons orange juice

club soda

dash grenadine syrup

slice of fresh pineapple

1. Shake the juices together in a container with some shaved ice. Pour the mixture over ice cubes in a collins glass. Top with club soda. Add the grenadine, and garnish with the pineapple.

Serves 1.

Leo the Lion

1/2 scoop raspberry sherbet

1/2 cup orange juice

6 tablespoons club soda

1 orange slice

1 maraschino cherry

1. Put the sherbet and orange juice in a blender, and blend at medium-high speed for 15 seconds. Pour into a glass, and top with club soda. Garnish with the orange slice and cherry.

Serves 1.

NOTES

FROM THE PANTRY

Ingredients

Many items in the recipes for this cookbook are of such a general nature that they have not been specified in each recipe. The reader should note that the following specifics for ingredients have been assumed throughout the book, unless the recipe states otherwise.

Butter: lightly salted butter.
Eggs: large.
Flour: all-purpose flour, sifted once before the measurement.
Garlic: garlic cloves should be peeled.
Sugar: granulated sugar, unless another type of sugar is specified.

Definitions

The following definitions refer to terms used throughout this cookbook.

Clarified butter: Whole butter that has been allowed to melt slowly, allowing the milky solids to drift to the bottom of the pan, and the clear liquid to rise to the top. It's this clear, top liquid that is known as clarified butter. Clarified butter does not burn as easily as whole butter, and is preferred for sautéing delicate fish and chicken dishes, and for bread rounds or croutons. *Specific directions for making clarified butter are found on page 25.*

Roux: A thickening agent for creamy sauces. It is a combination of butter and flour cooked slowly together for several minutes before adding the liquid. Slow cooking eliminates the raw, pasty taste of uncooked flour, and prepares the flour granules for absorption of the liquid. Specific directions for making a roux are found in each recipe that uses one.

BIBLIOGRAPHY

American Heritage Magazine, the editors of. *The American Heritage Cookbook.* New York: American Heritage Press, 1964.

"Antique Hunters Comb Garrets of Farm Houses in Berkshire." *The Springfield Sunday Republican*, February 28, 1928.

Bass, Milton. "The Red Lion Inn." *The Berkshire Eagle*, July 29, 1973.

Beard, James. *American Cookery.* Boston: Little, Brown and Company, 1972.

Beeton, Mrs. Isabella. *Beeton's Book of Household Management.* London: S.O Beeton, 18 Bouverie St. E.C., 1861.

Begley, Sally. "Up Country." *The Berkshire Eagle*, December 3, 1973.

The Berkshire Eagle. 1934.

Berkshire Resort Topics. 1904.

Blake, Andrew. "Sweet Sculpture." *The Boston Sunday Globe*, March 26, 1978.

Byrne, Robert. *1911 Best Things Anybody Ever Said.* New York: Fawcett Columbine, 1988.

Chadwick, Mrs. J. *Home Cookery.* Boston: 1853.

Chapman, Gerard. *A History of The Red Lion Inn in Stockbridge, Massachusetts.* Stockbridge: The Red Lion Inn, 1987.

Chapman, Gerard. "Stockbridge Cat and Dog Fountain." *The Berkshire Eagle*, September 5, 1978.

Child, Julia, et al. *Mastering the Art of French Cooking.* New York: Alfred A. Knopf, 1966.

Cobbett, William. *A Year's Residence in the United States of America*, 1819.

Day, Charles. *Hints on Etiquette*, 1844.

Doherty, Robert H., ed. *The First Ladies Cook Book.* New York: Parents' Magazine Press, 1966.

Earle, Alice Morse. *Stage-Coach and Tavern Days.* New York: The Macmillan Company, 1900.

Early, Eleanor. *New England Cookbook.* New York: Random House, Inc., 1954.

Field, Mrs. Stephen Johnson. *Statesmen's Dishes and How to Cook Them.* 1890.

Forbes, Allan and Ralph M. Eastman. *Taverns and Stagecoaches of New England.* Boston: Printed by the State Street Trust Co., The Rand Press, 1954.

Franklin, Benjamin. "Homespun." *The Gazetteer*, January 2, 1766.

Harger, L.W. "First Red Lion Inn was Built in 1773." (name of newspaper unknown) Pittsfield, Massachusetts: June 7, 1912.

Leonard, Jonathan Norton and the editors of Time-Life Books. *American Cooking: New England*. New York: Time-Life Books, 1970.

Leslie, Eliza. *Miss Leslie's Complete Cookery*. Philadelphia: E. L. Carey & A. Hart, 1837.

National Society of The Colonial Dames of America. *Old Inns of Connecticut*. Hartford, CT, The Prospect Press, 1937.

O'Connell, Jean. "Christmas Every Day at Gumdrop Square." *The Springfield Sunday Republican*, December 19, 1976.

Owens, Carole. *The Berkshire Cottages, A Vanishing Era*. Englewood Cliffs, NJ: Cottage Press, Inc., 1984.

Parker, James Reid. "Down From the Mountain." *The New Yorker*, September 4, 1948.

The People of Stockbridge, Massachusetts. *The Stockbridge Story 1739 - 1989*. Stockbridge, Massachusetts, 1989.

"Red Lion Inn Totally Destroyed by Fire This Morning." *The Pittsfield Evening Journal*, August 31, 1896.

Rombauer, Irma S. and Marion Rombauer Becker. *Joy of Cooking*. Indianapolis: The Bobbs-Merrill Company, Inc., 1964.

Root, Waverly and Richard de Rochemont. *Eating in America, A History*. New York: William Morrow and Company, Inc., 1976.

Sedgwick, Henry Dwight. *Memoirs of an Epicurean*. New York: The Bobbs-Merrill Company, 1942.

Sedgwick, Sarah Cabot and Christina Sedgwick Marquand. *Stockbridge 1739-1939, A Chronicle*. Great Barrington, Massachusetts: The Berkshire Courier, 1939.

Simmons, Amelia. *American Cookery*. Reprint of the First Edition, New York, 1958.

The Springfield Union, September 12, 1943.

Stowe, Harriet Beecher. *Oldtown Folks, A Story of New England*. Reprint of 1869 edition, AMS Press, 1969.

Treadway, Heaton. *The Tale of the Lion*. Stockbridge, Massachusetts, The Red Lion Inn.

Tree, Christina, "A Passion for Inns," *The Boston Globe*, November 28, 1971.

Trollope, Frances. *Domestic Manners of the Americans*. Edited by Donald Smalley. New York: Alfred A. Knopf, 1949.

Willan, Anne. *Great Cooks and Their Recipes From Taillevent to Escoffier*. Boston: Little, Brown and Company, 1992.

The Women of General Foods Kitchens. *The General Foods Cookbook*. New York: Random House, 1959.

SUBJECT INDEX

RECIPE INDEX

ABOUT THE OWNERS

Jack and Jane Fitzpatrick are owners of the historic Red Lion Inn in Stockbridge, Massachusetts — a wonderful country inn filled with antiques. Their daughter Nancy Fitzpatrick is married to Lincoln Russell and has a son Casey. Their other daughter, Ann, is married to Richard Brown and they have a son Alexander.

COUNTRY LION AGENCY

CRAIG HAMMELL

ABOUT THE CHEF

Chef Steven Douglas Mongeon has been executive chef of The Red Lion Inn for twelve years. He is a graduate of The Culinary Institute of America, and a Culinary Instructor at Berkshire Community College. In addition, he is a member of the Berkshire County Chapter of the American Culinary Federation, where he has served as Vice President for two terms, and is the recipient of numerous professional and culinary awards. Chef Mongeon is married and has three children.

ABOUT THE AUTHOR

Suzi Forbes Chase is a writer with an extensive culinary background. She has attended *Ecole de Cuisine La Varenne* in Paris, and Peter Kump's Cooking School and The China Institute in New York, as well as wine courses in France and the United States. She has written thirteen travel/history books, numerous magazine articles, collaborated on several travel guides, and is a member of the American Society of Journalists and Authors. She and her husband live in Stockbridge and New York.